The GOD
of
SECOND
CHANCES

The GOD of SECOND CHANCES

STEPHEN ARTERBURN

TYNDALE

Tyndale House Publishers, Wheaton, Illinois

THE GOD OF SECOND CHANCES
Copyright © 1997 by Stephen Arterburn
All rights reserved. International copyright secured.

Library of Congress Cataloging-in-Publication Data
Arterburn, Stephen, 1953–
    The God of Second Chances / Stephen Arterburn
      p. cm.
    ISBN 1-56179-717-0
    1. Arterburn, Stephen, 1953–.   2. Christian
biography—United States.
    3. Christian life.   I. Title.
    BR1725.A79A3   1997
    277.3'082—dc20
    [B]   96-43831
                                       [CIP]

A Focus on the Family book published by Tyndale House
Publishers, Wheaton, Illinois.

This author is represented by the literary agency of Alive
Communications, 1465 Kelly Johnson Blvd., Suite 320,
Colorado Springs, CO 80920.

Unless otherwise noted, Scripture quotations are from the HOLY
BIBLE, NEW INTERNATIONAL VERSION.® Copyright ©
1973, 1978, 1984 by the International Bible Society. Used by permission of Zondervan Publishing House. All rights reserved. Quotations labeled *The Message* are from *The Message: The New
Testament in Contemporary English*, by Eugene H. Peterson, ©
1993 by NavPress. Used by permission. All rights reserved.

Focus on the Family books are available at special quantity dis-
counts when purchased in bulk by churches, schools, or
libraries. For more information, contact: Focus on the Family,
Educational Resources, P.O. Box 15379, Colorado Springs, CO
80935, or phone 1-800-932-9123.

This book was previously published under the title
Surprised By God.

Cover design by Carrie L. Ketcham
Cover image by ©1999 PhotoDisc, Inc.

Printed in the United States of America
99 00 01 02 03 04/10 9 8 7 6 5 4 3 2 1

ACKNOWLEDGMENTS

My thanks to Rob Wilkins and Terry Whalin, who
helped me turn my thoughts and notes into a book.
They helped to take my stories and ideas and
transform them into a message of hope.

Thanks also to the entire Focus on the Family
Publishing team. I appreciate them walking so
closely with me through this process.

CONTENTS

A SOUL DAMAGED

PART ONE

CHAPTER ONE

THE JOURNEY OF LIFE

TWO PATHS *to* CHOOSE FROM

They called it the golden egg. I called it the Big One. It was Easter, and I was a three-year-old on an egg hunt. This was serious business. Candy, you must understand, was an extremely important part of my life. A lot of children had come with the same intent I had—to gather up as much candy and as many eggs as possible. I couldn't count at that time, but I remember thinking, *There must be a hundred kids here.*

Because I was so young, my mom let me watch the organizers hide the colored eggs and chocolates on the green, rolling field where the hunt would take place. Before long, I had spotted the man with the Big One—a jumbo-sized, cream-filled chocolate egg wrapped in gold foil. He was off to the side of the field, jamming the prized egg into a hole where a water faucet pipe came up through the ground. I may have been only three, but I wasn't a fool. I knew an inside tip when I saw one. Call it a competitive edge in the bunny-eat-bunny world of Easter egg hunts.

All the kids were herded behind the starting line. Most of the others were much older and bigger than me—but not wiser. With the word "Go!" the hunt started, and I made a beeline for the Big One. It didn't matter how many colored eggs or chocolates laid in my path; I did not stop to pick up these lesser, almost meaningless morsels. My legs, being puny three-year-old models, could not take me there fast enough. Relatively soon, however, I reached my destination. I glanced around. I was alone. The egg was mine, all mine.

But as I reached my hand into the shallow hole, my peewee face formed an expression you see only in old Hitchcock movies.

Huh? There's nothing here. The hole is empty.

Furiously, my little hand searched again and again for what I knew was to be mine. It was not there. I couldn't believe it. I put my basket down and tried the other hand, as if perhaps the egg were there but I had lost the ability to feel with my right hand. My left hand also seemed to be numb, since I again came up empty. I lay down on the grass and peered into the six-inch hole. I wasn't going to move until I found it. I started digging and pulling grass around that hole, but nothing I did uncovered the golden egg I had seen placed there.

At three, I wasn't able to consider the possibility that the man had moved the egg after I turned and walked back toward the starting line. I continued to search frantically, while precious minutes slipped away and the other kids gathered up hand-fuls of goodies.

A loud scream from across the field broke my concentration. In an old oak tree, between two branches that hung low enough for kids to reach, one of the children had found the Big One. Lesley Waters. I still remember her name. As I ran across the field in disbelief, fake green grass flew from my otherwise empty basket. Looking around, I saw that all the other children's baskets were full to overflowing. When I spotted Lesley with the Big One, I started to cry. My mom came and made my brothers give me some of their candy. Talk about adding insult to injury—now I had a small pile of hand-me-down candy.

From the certainty of a sweet and calculated victory came the bitter taste of defeat. Still, the day wasn't a total loss, for I learned a valuable lesson: That which promises to bring happiness and ful-fillment often leaves us empty. Unfortunately, it was a lesson I've had to learn over and over.

؛

Chiune Sugihara had a dream. Growing up in Japan during the early 1900s, he wanted to be an ambassador to Russia. Chiune studied hard, learn-ing seven languages. A steady and conscientious worker and a capable linguist, he gradually made his way up the bureaucratic ladder. By the late 1930s, he was named the Japanese consul to

Lithuania. Although he was inching closer to his
dream, he was still considered a low-level civil ser-
vant. But that would change, he knew. Nothing, he
believed, could keep him from his dream.

~

Most of us spend considerable time and energy
searching for the Big One—whatever it is we think
will bring lasting joy and satisfaction. We dream
about it, sweat over it, even do without other,
smaller things in its pursuit. For we know once we
have achieved, possessed, owned, romanced, or con-
quered the Big One, our lives, once and for all, will
be happy and fulfilling. This is true of most humans,
not just three-year-olds on Easter egg hunts.

We desperately do not want to live our lives
unloved, unknown, and feeling "unalive." We
search for meaning, pleasure, esteem, recognition,
and freedom. These are not bad goals. The problem
is how we try to achieve these goals, what *path* we
take to attain them. We see the Big One, and we're
sure it will bring us happiness. It might be in a pile
of money, in the heart of a future spouse, on a
nameplate on a desk, on the eighteenth green of a
posh golf course—or, for that matter, anything that
represents success in terms the world understands.

Proverbs 14:12 addresses our quest for fulfillment: "There is a way that seems right to a man, but
in the end it leads to death." Often this death does
not mean a literal trip to the grave but a spiritual

death, which includes perpetual longing, emptiness, and futility. It is the feeling of a three-year-old in the giant, green field, holding an empty basket with fake green grass stuck between two of your six teeth. The pursuit of the Big One has not only been a waste of time, but an utter embarrassment. You end up hating Lesley Waters, even though you would rather not. You just can't stand the way she dances around the oak tree.

The "way that seems right to a man" might be called the broad path. It is full of all the pleasures of this world. Here, you find money, sex, and power, which promise happiness but deliver deep emptiness. What seems so certain to fulfill you turns out to be an illusion. In the end, the price you pay is your soul.

God desires more for our lives. He wants us to travel the narrow path, which brings fulfillment and meaning. The Bible tells us that those who follow this road must be committed to self-sacrifice, delayed gratification, responsibility, and integrity.

Part of the problem Christians face is embracing the promises of God. We often mistakenly think of Him as the Great Killjoy, performing acts of magic, complete with thunder and fanfare, to keep us miserably on our knees. Actually, though, Jesus said that a life committed to following Him will bring joy, freedom, intimacy, and genuine satisfaction. He said, "I have come that they may have life, and have it to the full" and "If you obey my commands, you will remain in my love. . . . I have told you this so that my joy may be in you and that your joy may be complete" (John 10:10; 15:10–11).

But the fulfillment of these promises comes by walking a path we would never expect. The path to joy is a narrow one, and God continues to surprise us along the way. As Jesus said, "Enter through the narrow gate. For wide is the gate and broad is the road that leads to destruction, and many enter through it. But small is the gate and narrow the road that leads to life, and only a few find it" (Matthew 7:13–14).

With so much hope available to all of us who struggle, it is sad that we often find ourselves in seemingly hopeless situations. We're bombarded with endless pitches for that *something* that's "guaranteed" to bring true happiness, and we can no longer hear the still, small voice of God leading us. We're promised quick fixes and instant solutions: Buy this car. Try this pill. Chant this mantra. Use this diet. Pursue this relationship. It's incredible how many people tell us how to live our lives and profess to have the inside track on the truth. And the majority of these people and their intricate systems of knowledge reject the truth of God.

There is one great truth and one great lie. The great truth is that God loves us, and through Him we find ultimate meaning and fulfillment. The great lie says we can control our own destinies and find contentment on our own. When we leave the truth—the narrow and grace-filled path of God's love—we pursue the lie, the broad and deadly path, the lovely mirage of self-determination. The lie prompts us to try to "make life happen" by our own devices and schemes.

Unfortunately, no matter how closely we follow God, none of us is immune to straying. Even though we know better, we take the broad path once again, partly because the narrow path seems so demanding. Nevertheless, to find true joy and meaning in life, we must return to the truth and base our lives on the one source of guidance that never fails—God's Word, the Bible.

∽

Through hard work and loyalty, Chiune Sugihara was one step away from his goal. As he began to work as the Japanese consul in Lithuania, he dreamed about his next promotion and the realization of his lifelong career goal: becoming the ambassador to Russia. But suddenly, there was a hitch in his plan—World War II.

Early one morning in the summer of 1940, Chiune woke up to find a group of people gathered around his house. They were Jews desperate to escape Poland as Hitler's army encroached. It soon became clear that he was their only chance to avoid the death camps. They needed him to issue visas, which would allow them to flee across the Baltic Sea to Japan and from there pursue freedom elsewhere. The lives of these Jews depended upon him.

Three times Chiune cabled his superiors asking permission to write the visas, and three times he was denied. The Japanese government was aligning itself with Hitler. Chiune faced a difficult decision. Would he stick to his own agenda and pursue his dream? Or would he seek to meet the needs of these desperate people? Would he risk his family's safety for the possible freedom of these strangers?

❧

Those of us who call ourselves Christians know that the broad path steers us away from the one true God of the universe and toward the false gods of this world. These gods lead us to artificial joys, like mirages in the desert that deceive us with promises to quench our thirst. We know better. We have been warned thousands of times. Yet so often, we veer off course. Why? Because there is some satisfaction even in what is fake. Our needs feel met—temporarily. It is no wonder we have a hard time staying on the narrow path to fulfillment and freedom. The world with its fake truth and coun-terfeit promises seems so appealing, so real, so accessible. Yet, as I noted earlier, Proverbs tells us that this path *always*—not *maybe* or *sometimes*— ends in death and destruction. Settling for the mediocre existence of a counterfeit life cuts us off from the surprising grace of God.

We all know people who look so good, so together. In our jealousy, we want what they have. What we don't know is that their happiness is shallow. We follow our perceptions of them instead of God's reality. We pursue the image that someone presents of the "good life," crafting our idols. In the end, however, we find out the person is morally bankrupt, and the path has led us to destruction.

I once heard a story of a farmer who decided to sell his sheep at market. On the way there, his truck caught on fire. He stopped immediately, lowered the truck's ramp, and led his sheep to safety. As he and the little flock stood near the burning vehicle, one of the sheep broke from the group, and walked back up the ramp and into the fire. The rest of the sheep followed this "leader" to their deaths.

With our propensity to follow others who lead us astray, is it any wonder the Bible says that we are like sheep?

⁂

Writing in longhand, Chiune Sugihara began to issue visas for the Jews who sought his help. For 28 days during that summer in 1940, with only a few breaks for sleep or food, he wrote visa after visa after visa. At night his wife would have to massage the cramps out of his hand. Each visa, he knew, would allow a whole family to find freedom.

Eventually, the Japanese removed Chiune from his job. Yet even as he was on the train to Berlin, he continued to write visas. He shoved them through the window of the train and handed them to the desperate Jews. During Chiune's final moments in Lithuania, a young Jewish man ran alongside the train yelling, "Chiune Sugihara, we will never forget you." They never did. Chiune Sugihara made the decision for service rather than self-preservation.

∾

In the journey of life, it matters tremendously which path we choose. Many people pursue the gods of this age—money, power, possessions, control, comfort, pleasure—and worship at their altars, whatever the cost. We seek to find freedom in these gods but end up trapped. There has never been an age that 2 Peter 2:19 described more accurately: "They promise them freedom, while they themselves are slaves of depravity—for a man is a slave to whatever has mastered him." Our society, while claiming to be enlightened and progressive, is shackled with addiction, moral decay, violence, despair, and apathy. The age of self-fulfillment has led to self-destruction.

Despite the pain the broad road brings, far too few of us spend enough time walking the narrow path, where real joy is available. By following Jesus, we can know the truth and have it set us free. But living by freedom and grace is not easy because it takes discipline. It requires that we have faith in Jesus and give our lives over to Him.

None of us likes to give up control. We would rather buy the lies of the world than follow in the freedom of truth. Some of us buy the lie of *fate:* We are simply born a certain way, and our genes keep us from following the narrow path. Others buy the lie of *religion:* We would rather hold on to rules, hiding behind rituals and lists of do's and don'ts, than be in a loving relationship with an awesome and often unpredictable God. Others buy the lie of *having it all:* We want temporary satisfaction rather than eternal fulfillment. We often split ourselves in two by trying to straddle both paths. We end up confused and torn, never satisfied with what we have, and never experiencing what we truly need.

Even for the most sincere Christians, life is filled with struggle, doubt, and frustration. If you don't struggle, if your faith has freed you from all worry and anxiety, you don't need this book. If you have become a Christian and everything has magically worked out for you, then I have nothing to offer. If you are completely immune from sexual temptation or if your attitude toward money and material possessions has never been a problem, don't bother reading on. This is a book for fellow strugglers who, even as they limp, want to move toward joy.

For most men and women, there comes a time when they decide to stop settling for mediocre lives. With growing disdain and regret, they search for something better, richer, deeper. Many people will give up everything to find authentic joy, a life full of purpose and integrity.

You may be there. You may be ready to let go of what is known and take a journey into the unknown—a journey full of fears, thrills, servant-hood, and gratitude. You may be ready to give up the second best and seek the heights and depths of an unburdened relationship with God through Jesus Christ. You may be ready for life, real life.

෴

Upon his return to Japan, Chiune Sugihara was fired from the Japanese Foreign Ministry. He spent his remaining years eking out a living as a lightbulb peddler, selling in seven different languages. He never realized his lifelong dream of becoming an ambassador to Russia.

෴

Some misguided leaders tell us that following Christ brings one joyous experience after another. But following after God, the *real* one, often involves suffering, surrender, and patience. There are plenty of reasons that the path Jesus described is called *narrow*. In seeking after purpose and ful-fillment, we often feel restrained by such pesky realities as *conscience* and *morality*. Because we follow God, we give up control of ourselves and often feel totally out of control.

But then the truth strikes us. We are surprised to discover that while it is not a pain-free existence, following God leads to real joy. By relinquishing self-control and giving ourselves away in the love of God, we find ourselves experiencing deep and sustaining satisfaction. It is the path that, by the power and grace of God, can move us *through* pain to peace. It is the path that, by following after what is real and eternal, can bypass the false gods of this world, which ultimately bring only emptiness. It is the path that, through obedience, sets us free.

Sadly, though, it is the path seldom followed. I should know. I am a prodigal son from a family of prodigal sons. My parents, who lived out a deep faith, had three sons leave the narrow path to pursue their own ways. My dad made the biblical father of the prodigal son look like a rookie. My brothers and I had to find out for ourselves that the broad path, which looks so good, is a pain-filled lie. Even though each of us eventually came back, we did not escape the consequences of our sin.

This book is, in part, my life story. It tells how I left the narrow path as outlined in the Bible to pursue the false gods of our age and how my "successes" became bitter failures. In Part One, I describe those pursuits that led me (and lead many others) off the narrow path and away from the joy that comes from following God. In Part Two, I outline the flip side of those empty pursuits—the choices and endeavors that bring ultimate healing, wholeness, and fulfillment.

By chasing after self-interests, I became spiritually and emotionally bankrupt. Shocked by the consequences of self-obsessive sin, I even became suicidal. By describing my bad decisions, I hope to show that the self-serving, self-gratifying wide road is always a deadend. I hope to save some from needless pain. But the story does not end with myself. It goes on to tell of God's incredible and surprising grace. By simply trusting Him, He has stunned me by turning my pain into purpose, my desperation into hope, my broken dreams into a vision of His kingdom. Remarkably and supernaturally, He has restored my soul.

Yet even now, as my heart longs to follow God, I often find myself wandering away from Him. In a thousand ways, pursuing a thousand subtle lies, I leave the narrow path, only to return with a sense of desperation, pain, and emptiness. While that might disappoint you, it is reality—for myself and every imperfect Christian I know.

The Bible says that we are to "encourage one another daily, as long as it is called Today, so that none of you may be hardened by sin's deceitfulness" (Hebrews 3:13). As a man who has traveled the appealing but destructive wide path, I hope this book will encourage you to follow Jesus on the narrow road to joy.

You will find the way to fulfillment and freedom in the pages of this book. I know this because I copied the guidelines out of another book—the Bible. They have always been there, but sometimes it's hard for us to see what is so plainly before us. Sometimes it takes being trapped and empty before we're willing to take another look at the truth that has been there all along.

&

Years after his death, Chiune Sugihara's family was interviewed by a newspaper. When asked why he had defied his government and written the visas for the Jews, his family told about Chiune's commitment to Jesus Christ. When he was young, he accepted Christ as his Savior. Years later, when surrounded by the desperate Jews, it was God's still, small voice that he heard. He had no choice but to help, to do whatever he could. His widow, Yukiko, expressed it this way: "It was his character that he was always giving priority to someone else, [to] what they needed."

Chiune's family all said that he had found fulfillment and was satisfied with his life, even though he never became ambassador to Russia. By listening to God's call, by choosing the narrow road, Chiune found a deep joy and fulfillment that no position or prestige could bring. He was, his family said, more than just a lightbulb peddler who could sell in seven languages. The 10,000 Jews he saved from extermination, as well as their 40,000 descendants, would no doubt agree.

CHAPTER TWO

FALSE GODS

*L*IES DISGUISED *as* TRUTH

On the broad paths of destruction, the road signs are attractive. Paradise Just Ahead. Food for the Soul. Entering the State of Bliss. The billboards, glittering in golden light, say: Take, Eat, Enjoy, Gather. The absence of speed limits and lack of Yield signs promise excitement.

And although the messages are all lies, they are, in the words of Bruce Springsteen, "brilliant disguises." How can anything that looks so good, promises so much, and evokes such powerful longings be anything but right? Even if the messages are not entirely true, we rationalize, who cares as long as they work? It is easy to buy into lies without recognizing the true price: our souls.

I know. Early in my life, I began to believe lies. I believed there were no consequences for moving away from God. I believed that pursuing pleasure now would not produce pain later. I believed I had to please myself since I couldn't please God. Even though my parents were devout and authentic Christians, I wanted *more* from life. I saw God as a dreadful and supernatural being who had to be coaxed and manipulated into blessing. I never left the church; in fact, I remained active. But I also tested the waters of the world. I was like a toddler pushing the boundaries of his parents' rules to see just how far he could go without getting in trouble. If I did *this*—say, get drunk with the guys after a high school football game—would God punish me? And then, when I got away with that, I felt more confident to try some other sin. I would think, *See, I did that, and nothing terrible happened. No lightning bolts from heaven, no illnesses, no calamities.* It's too bad that God's consequences aren't always immediate.

In my heart, I believed God would never allow me to suffer irreversible damage, that He would reel me back in His great and harsh love before I had set a price on my soul. So before long, I was living with one foot in the church and one foot in the world. It was not uncommon for me to sing a moving solo about God's love the morning after a night of riotous, prodigal-style living. I was surprised that God allowed me to get away with it. I mistakenly equated His silence with distance or inattention.

Desperate for acceptance and something to numb my pain and confusion, I sought to charm whomever I could. I relished being the life of the party, quick with a joke or glib comment that would make everyone smile. And to some extent, I was good at it. I won awards, friendships, praise, and promotions. Well into my young adult life, I believed the most deadly lie of all—that *I* was responsible for my own happiness.

Trouble in Paradise

In 1825, long before Hawaii met its first tourist, the U.S. schooner the *Dolphin* set out on a mission of justice. The captain was ordered to bring to trial a group of sailors who had led a mutiny on a ship called the *Globe*. The *Globe*'s captain had had his head rather unceremoniously split in two with an ax. The mutineers, who settled on the island now known as Hawaii, believed they could live in that paradise without experiencing any negative consequences for their behavior. The crew of the *Dolphin* set out to prove them wrong.

What interests me in this story is not whether the mutineers were brought to justice or not (eventually they were), but the psychological drama that played out. When the *Globe* arrived on the shores of Hawaii, thousands of dark-skinned natives greeted the boats. For a while, the crew feared for their lives, since they were far outnumbered by the natives. What would these island people do to the pale-skinned strangers? Because they were in desperate need of supplies, the crew decided to risk their lives by going ashore. Upon landing, an amazing thing happened: The natives began to treat the crew members like gods. In fact, very little was required of them to gain worship. First, the islanders were impressed by the crew's fair skin, glimmering brass buttons, and ship with huge sails that harnessed the power of the wind. Second, the crew perpetrated a lie: They convinced the islanders that, although outnumbered, they could easily overpower them with supernatural force. The natives never once questioned the authority of these pale-skinned "gods."

Penned into a journal of the voyage that day was this profound entry: "So ready is the human mind to receive for truth, what it cannot comprehend . . . though it may be at variance with everything in nature or reason." While I don't believe these crewmen possessed superior intelligence, they had superior knowledge about the ways of the world. For them, truth was simply a tool for power and control.

In the years that have passed since the voyage of the *Globe*, little has changed in the minds of men and women. Much of what is passed off as truth, or at least knowledge, is motivated by a desire to control and possess. Truth, then, is defined by abusive leaders as not so much a matter of what is "right or wrong," but rather what "works for me." Often we follow "truth" not because we are morally or spiritually convicted but on the basis of how many letters are behind the name of the "expert" who formulated the theory. We find ourselves believing many so-called truths even though they may go against everything we've been taught.

We like to call ourselves sophisticates. We believe in scientific theory and read the *Wall Street Journal*. We subscribe to the theory, secretly or not, that humankind is evolving and that we are far superior to our brutish and superstitious ancestors. We smirk when we read how they worshiped gods—those deaf, dumb, and mute pieces of wood and gold. We scoff, *How could those people really bow down to a golden calf?*

Yet at the same time, without even knowing it, we are on our knees before more subtle (but just as real) false gods. They are the "isms" of our day: workaholism, as if the fruit of endless labors will finally bring satisfaction; or legalism, as if being good and performing flawlessly will secure peace; or intellectualism, as if we could get so smart that we would finally feel fulfilled; or materialism, as if some *thing* could give us joy.

The first step onto the broad path is to follow one of these false gods—lies brilliantly disguised as the truth, but lies nonetheless.

Embraced by the Lies

The most dangerous kind of lie comes clothed in the name of truth and sold as religion. Since it was published, Betty Eadie's book *Embraced by the Light* has spent many, many months on the *New York Times* bestseller lists, both hardcover and paperback. It has sold millions of copies. The book tells of a near-death, out-of-body experience that the author claims she had, even though she supplies no documentation that she died and was revived.

On the basis of this subjective experience alone, Eadie has become a contemporary expert on religion. She has made herself a trusted source on such realities as heaven, hell, God, Jesus, and just about everything else. She has accumulated enormous power. People by the thousands (even some Christians) are calling her a prophet. I watched her on television one day as she told a packed room of people her story of dying, going toward a light, seeing Jesus, and entering heaven. The audience was spellbound by her words.

After reading her book and listening to her lectures, I see her ability to transform lies into the "truth" as a way to win the trust of her listeners. In one manner or another, in fact, all false gods use this time-tested formula. It is a formula for disaster as old as the serpent in the Garden.

Each enticement away from God's narrow road and onto the broad path begins with the same words the serpent used: "Did God really say . . . ?" (Genesis 3:1). In order to believe a lie, we must first stop believing the truth. More often than not, this deception is not a blatant dismissal of the truth but a subtle distortion of it. The most effective lie is often the one that travels the shortest distance from the truth.

In her philosophy, Betty Eadie in effect asks the same question, "Did God really say . . . ?" If God—this "warm, embracing light"—is a God of love, would He send anyone to hell? Did Jesus, who was so gentle, really say He was the *only* way to heaven? The unspoken reply is, "Of course not." But God's truth is often a hard truth. He tells us that by ourselves we are helpless, hopeless, and doomed by our sin. Although God provides a way out of this dilemma, it is not by doing an end-run around these hard realities. Jesus, too, experienced the hardness of God's truth on the cross. The sinless One took on sin for us. He has asked us to pick up our crosses and follow Him on the narrow path.

False gods are appealing because they cast doubt on the hard realities: "Did God really say . . . ?" The hook always appeals to our selfish interests with a lie. "You will not surely die" were the serpent's next words (Genesis 3:4). Eadie—and many others—offers us a god who tells us the things we *want* to hear rather than the things we *need* to hear. The apostle Paul said it this way: "For the time will come when men will not put up with sound doctrine. Instead, to suit their own desires, they will gather around them a great number of teachers to say what their itching ears want to hear" (2 Timothy 4:3).

With the lure of false gods come three primary lies: (1) humans are basically good; (2) God would never punish us; and (3) we can, by our own efforts, be like God. Eadie is no exception among the false gods; she is an expert at tickling ears. She believes that each person, instead of being born with a sinful nature, is born with goodness in his heart. Even the most blatant "sinner," she believes, is accomplishing something good. My favorite story of hers, because of its absurdity, is about the man who chose to be a drunk. Instead of seeing the man as a person trapped by a powerful addiction, Eadie postulates that he is really a hero. Before he was even born, she theorizes, he decided to be a drunk. As a drunk, he knew he would lie passed out in front of a prominent attorney's office. The attorney, forced to see this helpless man, would then be able to maintain his love and compassion for needy people. Instead of wasting his life, this drunk was actually *giving* his life as a sacrifice so the attorney would remain sensitive to the needs of others.

Eadie's message contains the same power offered by the serpent and all the other false gods to follow: You can be like God. Eadie says it doesn't matter which god you follow because in the end that god will embrace you in the light of heaven. In essence, she says there is no one true God, so you can live your life however you choose. You control your own destiny.

The same is true with all of the false gods of our age, whether they be in the form of material-ism, hedonism, moralism, or any other philosophy.

The first step in the worship of false gods is exchanging the truth for lies. Once truth is discarded, anything can be believed.

The Old Testament prophet Isaiah issued a powerful warning to those who turn people from the truth: "Woe to those who call evil good and good evil, who put darkness for light and light for darkness, who put bitter for sweet and sweet for bitter" (5:20). Truth, the false gods tell us, is relative—what's good for me may be bad for you, and vice versa. In our age, the worst thing you can be labeled is "intolerant." Yet relative truth, by its very nature, is an oxymoron. How can two opposing ideas be true? Either there is one absolute truth or there is no truth at all.

The truth of the Bible does not change according to the situation or circumstances; it defines and weeds out all falsehood. And it is an uncomfortable truth that speaks hard things about the nature of reality, God, and people. Biblical truth maintains that only by the life and death of Jesus Christ can we receive salvation from God. We can do nothing through our own efforts, abilities, and power to save ourselves. We must accept those hard facts before the truth can ever set us free.

Lies Along the Narrow Path

It is not only self-proclaimed spiritual gurus, the heathen, and the power-hungry who believe and practice the lies of this world. Some of the most dangerous truth-twisting I know is done within what is supposed to be the body of Christ, the church. Claiming to lead us on the narrow path of truth, some of these people take us on dangerous, dead-end excursions.

There is a temptation for Christians to say it doesn't really matter what we do because grace covers us, and even if we are misled we are still covered by Christ's blood. That is the beginning of the lie—in such a profound truth. It's essential to realize that any time we leave the narrow path, we face death. Maybe not physical death, but a death to the new life that God desires for us.

Within the church, false teachers create a toxic faith. By departing from the hard truth (often quite subtly), they often cause the people they shepherd to lose their love for God and turn their backs on the church. Unfortunately, many of us are too willing to believe whatever people tell us—especially if they claim to be doing the will of God. The Bible says that we must be shrewd as snakes (Matthew 10:16). When it comes to believing what others say, we must be discerning and disciplined, filtering out the truth from lies.

One of the biggest lies within the body of Christ claims that once we accept Christ, our lives will be free from problems. Mirroring our society's quest for painless, instant results, some misguided teachers say that Jesus is the answer and stop there. They never mention the inevitable spiritual struggles and sacrifices necessary to live a God-honoring life. In a way, people who teach a struggle-free Christianity put a perverse spin on the lie that man is basically good. Although they concede it is Christ's blood that washes us clean, they do not give enough credence to the pervasive nature of sin, even after we accept Christ as Savior. Even the apostle Paul struggled with this, saying, "I have the desire to do what is good, but I cannot carry it out. For what I do is not the good I want to do; no, the evil I do not want to do—this I keep on doing" (Romans 7:18–19). Paul understood the enormous power of sin.

Christianity doesn't promise that we will be free from the consequences of sin. In fact, Christians, of all people, should be the most aware of its deadliness. Instead of ignoring sin or downplaying its effects, Christians must deal with it through the power of Christ and in the name of love. That means a continual struggle because our flesh will constantly be at odds with our spirit.

Those who promise a life without problems create problems. The flip side of the lie is this: If you struggle, there must be something wrong with your faith. This is a dangerous mockery of grace.

Sheila was a new Christian who genuinely felt healed from her promiscuous past. Yet as the months passed, her euphoria was replaced by old temptations. Because she was told that she was supposed to be free from struggle, Sheila soon began to substitute her faith for religion—that is, rituals and a legalistic list of do's and don'ts. She tried to cover up her feeling that she was a "second-class" Christian by living up to everyone else's expectations: volunteering for service projects, attending every church event, and saying and doing all the right things. But her heart grew weary; secretly, she believed that God had failed her and that it was up to her to be "more spiritual." Within months, she was empty and confused—and back in bed with a new lover. To this day, she rejects the free love of God. If only she had been told of the reality of struggle and been helped through it, she might not have fallen away from her faith. Some would say Sheila never *really* found Christ. I say that a false religion and a toxic faith destroyed the relationship she began with Christ.

The Difference Between Free and Cheap

The idea that God takes away all of our problems has more than one deadly offspring. If we don't fall into the trap of legalism, then we can be tempted to believe that God should be our personal miracle worker. The Bible says if we have enough faith, then God will answer our prayer. That is true. But the truth gets subtly twisted when we believe God has a *responsibility* to heal on demand, whether it is a broken relationship, a diseased body, or a shattered dream. If we do not receive healing, the reasoning goes, then there must be sin in our lives that prevents God from granting our request.

My wife, Sandy, and I have some friends who are wonderfully devoted Christians. Their first daughter was born with a severe mental handicap that will force her to be dependent on her parents all her life. Their second child was born with a serious deformity. These tragedies occurred despite many prayers by the parents and family members that God would give them healthy children. Some Christians had the audacity to tell them that their children were born that way because of sin in the parents' lives. Can you imagine the pain that these hurtful comments caused this already suffering couple?

The Bible clearly teaches that illness and physical maladies are not always the result of anyone's sin; they happen so the work of God can be manifested in a person's life (see John 9:1–3). God is more interested in a person's faithfulness and maturity in the face of suffering than He is in preventing us from experiencing pain.

When we leave the path of God's truth, death always occurs. Sometimes, as our friends discovered, the death can be a loss of hope and trust in the community of Christ; other times, it may be actual death. More than 126 children have died over the past few years because their parents withheld medical treatment, convinced that God would heal.[1] The sickness of their parents' beliefs led to these children's deaths every bit as much as their physical diseases did.

The story of Michael Pacewitz is a story of death, but with an odd twist. It is an example of a church that was full of love but was, at the same time, badly misled. Michael, a discharged patient from a mental institution, began attending a church in Orange County, California. Despite being labeled a schizophrenic, Michael developed relationships within the church and, for the first time in his life, felt genuinely loved and accepted. Soon he started doing odd jobs around the church. He became a Christian, and people learned to trust Michael.

Then one day a naive young pastor told Michael, "Now that you have become a Christian, you are a new creature in Christ. All of the old things have passed away and all within you is new." He advised Michael to stop taking his medication, which he did. In a few days, tragedy struck. While he was baby-sitting the children of a lady in the church, Michael killed her three-year-old son.

Later, sitting in a jail cell being interviewed, Michael said, "When I drove a knife through that small baby's heart, I felt the hand of Satan guiding my hand. I felt that I was Satan."

In a schizophrenic delusion, he killed a child.

What had been a wonderful story of restoration and healing suddenly turned into a nightmare for a young man, a family with a dead child, and a naive pastor who now says he will never again tell anyone not to take their medication. Michael Pacewitz, once a thriving member of a church, now sits in prison. He will probably never be released from an institution of some kind.[2]

We need to use our God-given brains and stop victimizing people, whether it is with quick fixes and instant solutions or shallow answers that rob people of their faith. We must begin to realize that faith is a process and that struggle, doubt, and imperfection are not enemies of the gospel, but are often used by God to develop the faith He wants in each of us.

The Perfect-Mate Myth

The lies of the world have also infiltrated the church in the area of relationships. We believe, in our heart of hearts, in what I call the "Perfect-Mate Syndrome." This belief, which applies to both singles and married couples, goes something like this: "If I just had the right mate, then my life would be all right." This belief is incredibly ignorant. First, it assumes that we are good and it's our spouse (or lack of a spouse) who is the *real* problem. Second, it also infers that there is such a thing as a "perfect" spouse, one who is beyond the reach of sin.

This delusion keeps people from growing the way God wants them to. For those in difficult marriages, it prevents them from the hard work and commitment necessary to repair the relationship. And singles can be tempted to keep life on hold until the right spouse comes riding into his or her life. In either case, God is supposed to painlessly fix things by finally providing the *right* spouse. For God to ask us to stay and fix a marriage or for Him to deny us a spouse altogether seems cruel or unfair.

God is most concerned about our relationship with Him. If we are married, we will find that the way to keep the relationship stable and growing is to build our relationship with God—together and individually. If we do that, our marriage will be strengthened along with our soul. God wants our attitude to be, "I'm in this for the long haul. I'm going to dedicate myself to making this marriage last." This is how an active and true faith comes alive in a marriage that will be anything but perfect or close to paradise. Similarly, God wants the attitude of every faithful Christian single to be, "God, I'm Yours whether I have a spouse or not." Whatever your situation, God is sufficient to meet your needs.

Giving to Get

Our culture's emphasis on "getting what is ours" has created a dangerous attitude regarding service in the church. We sometimes serve because we expect to be blessed. While Scripture does promise that our lives will be fulfilled through serving God and one another, the truth has been subtly twisted—we expect our blessing as a *reward* or *payment*, not as a *gift*. There is a world of difference here. One mind-set demands from God; the other gratefully accepts.

People who serve only to receive blessings operate more under the law than under grace. They produce good works, believing they will be compensated with blessings from God. Because such people operate under the serpent's lie that they are basically good, they focus on service as being good work that *should* be rewarded by God. They tend to forget that this same reasoning dictates that sin deserves consequences (punishment).

In many churches, this belief is taken to an extreme in the area of financial giving. Many people are fed the lie that if they give their money to God, He will give them more back in return. One church leader convinced his parishioners to give 100 percent of their salary each January as a way of honoring God with their "first fruits." In principle that may not sound bad, but he went on to promise that by doing so, all of those who gave would receive more of God's fruit in return throughout the year. Only in our materialistic age could we imagine that God wants us to have a lot of money, and therefore we should give Him a little and wait for Him to make us rich. Yet there are millions who believe that if they have enough faith, God will reward them with financial blessings.[3] I wonder how many people have turned from Christ because their expectations were so out of line with reality.

The False Gods

Satan, the Bible tells us, is the father of lies. In fact, lies are the foundation, the starting point of his strategy. With glittering deceptions, his lies ask, "Did God really say . . . ?" Once we abandon truth, we open ourselves up for all kinds of lies. As we have seen, these lies tend to focus on the following: people are basically good; sin is not that bad; and people are more deserving of reward than punishment.

When we operate under these false premises, we are no longer completely dependent upon God. His grace becomes something we can manipulate, buy, or charm. And when life does not turn out exactly as we hope, we fall into the most devious lie of all—that we, by our own effort, can control the destiny of our lives. We become our own false gods. It is here that inward faith is turned into superficial religion, that loving grace is transformed into deadly law.

CHAPTER THREE

MATERIALISM

THE DESIRE *to* ACQUIRE

I still remember the night. I was 12 years old, and my best friend and my girlfriend—or should I say the girl I *wished* was my girlfriend—were leaving for camp. I had to stay home. My parents said they just didn't have the money to send me. Later in life, I would understand that my brother, who was six years older than me, wanted to go to college, and my parents were simply exercising priorities. But at that time, as I wailed in my bedroom, I felt like my dad and mom were poor, poorer than anyone in our home state of Texas.

The night before I was to be left behind, I cried heavy tears all over the picture I wanted to give my "girlfriend." I didn't want her to forget me. They were going all the way to Branson, Missouri, to Kamp Kanakuk for boys and Kamp Kanakomo for girls. I couldn't afford to make the trip, but I felt as if I couldn't afford *not* to be there. I knew I could easily miss my opportunity with this girl.

The camp was more than just another dude ranch. It was the world to me. And it wasn't just that I wanted to go have fun; I desperately wanted to fit in, to feel that I belonged somewhere. I didn't always feel that way at home. I was a sensitive child, and I knew my parents loved me, but there were some unhealthy dynamics going on in my family. My dad, a man of deep faith who genuinely loved his children, was not raised by a father who taught him how to relate emotionally. My mother was the one primarily saddled with raising the children since my dad traveled a lot. But she was struggling to deal with the suicide of her father, which happened when I was a year old. She did her best, but she never had the opportunity at that time to work through her confusion and loss (which she has subsequently done).

So I searched for a place to belong. And that year, as I stood on the brink of entering into a troubling adolescence, the place was a camp in Branson, Missouri. Because I did not get to go, one of my friends ended up being the one to kiss "my" girl. Combining that pain (a big deal at that age!) with the reason I couldn't go (my family couldn't afford it) reinforced a misconception that had taken root in my mind—money was something that could connect me to where I wanted to go and to who I wanted to be.

In retrospect, I realize we were not as poor as I thought. My father owned three fast-food restaurants and my mom owned and managed several beauty shops. We were certainly not wealthy, but my family's poverty was more in my mind than anything. I just always *felt* we were poor. None of us boys received an allowance, I had to wear hand-me-down clothes, and our family was rarely invited to the places that the "in" people went. Each year, for example, many of my friends' parents went to Padre Island for a Fourth of July week of fun and fireworks. Our family never got invited. Although the snub had more to do with the fact that my parents didn't drink alcohol (a main attraction of the week), I equated it to our finances. Worse, my less-than-mature mind made a fallacious spiritual connection: If God really loved me, I reasoned, He wouldn't want me to be a "second-class" citizen in a first-class world.

To hide my feelings of inadequacy and pain, I compensated by hanging out with people who looked successful and well-off. Deep down, I felt as if I could increase my worth by merely being in the presence of the successful. My first real girlfriend (after the other budding romance fizzled) was the daughter of a farmer who owned a significant amount of land. She was a delightful girl with many wonderful qualities, but my attraction started with her family's prosperity. My next girlfriend was also the daughter of a wealthy man in the area. I was drawn to her father's outward signs of success long before I discovered just how remarkable she was as a person.

This set a pattern that continued well into my

adult life—outward appearance was always at least as important as inward qualities, if not more important. I bought into the same lie that Hollywood and the Manhattan advertising agencies whisper, and sometimes scream, into our ears every day. I made decisions based on superficial, rather than spiritual, reasons.

My reactions were somewhat unusual. Often people who feel inadequate in a certain area seek out others who are even less adequate, hoping to look good by comparison. I did just the opposite. I hoped that by rubbing shoulders with the rich and successful, some good would rub off on me—or at least that people might think more highly of me for having influential connections.

Interestingly, my longing to succeed and attain material wealth did not prompt me to work hard to achieve it. My life during those years mirrored the title of the popular stage play *How to Succeed in Business Without Really Trying*. I was unmotivated, undisciplined, and hurting. In college, I graduated with a degree in elementary education—certainly not in the Fortune 500 top-10 money-making degrees. I chose that major partly because I could not decide what else to do and partly because I knew it was a fairly easy degree to obtain. Instead of working for things, I was always trying to figure out how to stumble into the winner's circle. And when it came to finding happiness, I was unwilling to shut the door on any possibility. I kept one foot in the world, with its potential riches, and one foot in the church, storing up heavenly treasures "just in case." In the end, I nearly split myself in two.

Although I always struggled with deep feelings of inadequacy, in truth I was gifted. This was a deadly combination. It kept me from discipline or repentance and left me feeling that I constantly had to perform. I could succeed without a great deal of effort. On the football field, I was the starting fullback. In church, I could knock the congregation out of the pews with my hard-driving solos. In school, I could crack an A without cracking a book. People told me they expected me to do great things. On top of all that, I was a comedian.

But in those rootless, early adult years, I soon discovered that I lacked what was necessary for real success—discipline and strong character. Even though I was buoyed by a scholarship and praise for my natural singing gifts, my dream of becoming a professional singer (musical comedy suited me) faded as soon as I ran into the walls of difficult theory and endless arpeggios. I quickly learned that I could not charm my way to success and riches. All the things I wanted so badly became elusive. I desperately desired what I couldn't have. Consequently, I became even more ensnared in the trap of materialism.

Aside from my parents, whom I found myself

resenting for their "poverty," I had no clear example of someone who was free from the power of money. Even my pastor, by example, taught me to choose money, power, and pleasure over the treasures of God's kingdom. Growing up, I attended a thriving Baptist church in which the pastor was experienced and educated, with a doctor of philosophy in theology degree—not a backwoods, hick preacher. He had a Ph.D. behind his name just in case anyone doubted that he knew, and had thoroughly studied, the truth. Indeed, he won many people to Christ.

Eventually, however, this man did not look for meaning and significance in the truth of the Bible. He ended up leaving his wife and children to marry one of the church members, a recently widowed and extremely rich woman. In addition to deserting his family, the pastor also abandoned our church, as if we were a cheap date and not the bride of Christ. His example deluded many of the church members—including me—as to what really matters in this life.

Lessons from a Salesman

Materialism has been a deep source of confusion for me. Even when I should have known better, and even when I was sincerely turning to God in faith, the pursuit of things has tripped me up. After college, which was a dreadful period of pain and numbness for me, I decided to go to seminary. I was broken and deeply repentant over my sin. I wanted to start over. Yet, once again, I fell into the trap of chasing after things.

Just before starting seminary, I bought my first house for $10,000 with a down payment of only $1,000. The monthly mortgage payment was $100. What a deal! I congratulated myself for being so financially astute. But a door-to-door salesman changed all that. He came one day selling carpet, which was my house's only real deficiency. Covering the floors was a harvest-gold-colored carpet that, over the years, had turned into more of a harvest-dirt color. The salesman showed me a sample of sea-foam green, stain-resistant, nylon-and-polyester blend carpet. I was hooked. I simply *had* to have it. It was the most beautiful piece of carpet I had ever seen.

I didn't have the money to pay for it, so the salesman arranged for credit. Before he was finished, I had a home with brand-new wall-to-wall carpet and a payment coupon book about as thick as *Webster's Dictionary*—something like $35 a month for the next 35 years. Lovely. But there was another problem. After I had this beautiful new carpet installed, I noticed how ratty my furniture looked. A furniture sale quickly resolved that problem. I filled my house with a desert wildflower design. All I had to do was agree to pay $45 a month for 45 years, or something like that. But then there was another problem. As I was munching Doritos on my desert wildflower sofa, I realized how poor the reception was on my television. To remedy the situation, I bought a state-of-the-art Sony TV.

So there I was, watching my new television on my new desert wildflower sofa, which sat on my new sea-foam green, stain-resistant, nylon-and-polyester carpet. From the desert to the sea, everything seemed perfect . . . until the bills started rolling in, one after the other. Along with the other debts that I had accumulated, these new bills put me over the top. I could not make the minimum payments. For a while, I fought off the creditors. Eventually, in a panic, I responded to an advertisement for a bill consolidation loan company. After filling out more forms than it takes to get into college and waiting longer than it takes for an IRS return, I was finally granted a loan. By pooling my debts and extending the payments until I was sure I would be a great-grandfather, I could make the minimum payment each month. *Eventually*—and I cannot stress the word enough—I was able to pay off all of my bills.

What I thought would bring me respect and comfort made me a slave. But I did not find out the worst of it for years to come. I was simply dealing with the *symptom*—a desire to acquire—and not the underlying pain and emptiness that made things so attractive to me in the first place.

Looking Good versus Being Good

I could have blamed it on the culture. God knows we live in a society obsessed with things. We compete with one another to see who can acquire the most things, and then we measure ourselves—more surely than by our height and weight and IQ—by the size of our pile of stuff. Television, billboards, and blimps bombard us with the message that if we are to be truly successful, we must have things. Possessions, the brightly packaged lie says, are capable of granting us power, respect, acceptance, and safety. The sales pitches tap into deeply felt needs and make us squirm until we have acquired.

I recently met a woman at a party who told me about all the products she has purchased from late-night television infomercials. The array of goods was truly amazing; she had everything from sonic-powered toothbrushes to stain removers, fishing lures to food dehydrators, hair-cutting devices to contraptions that would produce rock-hard abs (in just five days!). Even though she was single, she had purchased numerous tapes and kits promising the secret to a lasting and happy marriage. She said she needed to prepare herself.

This woman simply could not (or rather, *would*

not) resist. After sitting through one of these slickly produced "documentaries," complete with personal testimonies from doctors, social experts, and ordinary folk whose lives had been changed by this particular product, she would grab her credit card and pick up the phone. Most of the stuff she didn't need and rarely used, but she still kept buying. Her house became a shrine to the infomercial gods.

"They make it look so good, so vital," she told me. "After I watch one of those infomercials, I'm convinced I just can't get along without the product they're selling. I should know better, but somehow I just keep getting fooled."

It's easy to laugh. We could easily dismiss her with a silly title such as "The Infomercial Queen" and pass her off as an oddity. But she is more like you and me than we might first suspect. We may not stay up late at night and order power paint sprayers, but don't we all do the same thing in a different way? Don't we all believe deep down that if we could just have IT, then we would be truly fulfilled, or at least partially satisfied? Maybe IT is a new computer, a new house, a new car, a new (and higher-paying) job, or a new wardrobe. And isn't it also true that once you manage to buy IT, then IT, after a short period of time, is not enough and must be replaced by still another IT?

The cycle of materialism always ends in some form of addiction. What we thought would free us ends up enslaving us. If we are trapped in material-ism, we never own things—they own us. I know of a Christian doctor who bought a house with a pool. He had always dreamed of owning a pool, both for the pleasure and the status that it offered. But as he described it, the pool ceased to be just a thing; it became like some ravenous creature from a Stephen King novel. THE POOL made endless demands on this family's life: Feed me chlorine; get that leaf out of here; remove that algae; buy me pool toys; patch that crack; change my chemistry. There were, in fact, several months when the family did not feel free to travel because of THE POOL. Within just a few years, he sold the house, primarily because he no longer wanted a pool.

"I knew that when I reached the age of 70," he told a friend, "I didn't want to be best remembered for how clean I kept my pool."

What he had hoped would give his family plea-sure and relaxation in the end turned into a demanding taskmaster.

So it is with many things we insist we cannot do without. Materialism trapped me into equating money and things with value. I longed to be con-nected with "quality" people, the movers and shak-ers, the "in" people. Although I have never been rich, I did find a way to achieve success. While attending seminary, I finally found my professional niche. Having experienced so many problems in my own life, and having reconnected with God during my last year of college, I was able to help some people with their problems. I had become acquainted with a professional counselor, so I decided I wanted to get involved in counseling. Unlike my earlier aimless years, I became motivated.

I took a job at a psychiatric hospital for highly disturbed people. I began two nights a week on the night shift. I then moved to full-time evenings and then full-time days while I was pursuing a master's degree in counseling at the University of North Texas. Within two years, I was the chief therapist at the hospital. Unfortunately, the hospital was in danger of shutting down because it had trouble attracting enough patients. So I switched gears. I got involved in the business end of the hospital, working in public relations, media, and administration. The hospital experienced a remarkable turnaround.

Shortly thereafter, I was transferred to another hospital that the company owned in California. Two years after I had completed my graduate school program and nine years after I had taken my first job as a patient attendant, I was named senior vice president of the company, where I presided over one-third of the ownings of the company, which eventually made more than one-half of its profit. I was then hired away by another company, which was struggling to free itself from a pending bankruptcy, and my salary was doubled. At the age of 32, I was chairman of a quarter-billion-dollar company.

On the surface, I had broken through many of the barriers I'd felt during my childhood. Through hard work and good breaks, I had reached a level of success. Even though I truly desired a relationship with God, I placed great emphasis on appearances. I would wear Ralph Lauren Polo shirts—the ones with the little horse over the heart. I even owned a gold Rolex watch. For a long time, I felt good in my shirts and watch. To some extent, they defined who I was; they gave me a sense of power and control.

But somewhere along the way, something happened. I began to feel foolish. Those images of prosperity, which I had hoped would connect me with important people and give me a sense of belonging, left me feeling disconnected and broken. What I had long thought would bring fulfillment left me empty. I slowly became aware that instead of opening up relationships, those symbols of success actually separated me from others. In fact, the whole purpose of those things was to build barriers between myself and other people. They became false readings of where I was in the world. They put me above others rather than with them.

I was presenting an image that, in my heart, I despised. I began to struggle against the hold that materialism had on my life. For a long time, I neglected the deeper issues of my heart, such as envy, disappointment, greed, and anger, which were driving my materialism. Although I eventually gave up the Polo shirts and gold watch, I left the envy in my heart mostly untouched; in essence, I dealt with materialism by hiding it—by driving a beat-up car or denying what I still wanted. But materialism, I found, can still have a deep hold on us, even if we live in virtual poverty. We can experience our lust just as easily in a shabby Volkswagen as in a shiny Lamborghini.

Materialism is one of the most deadly diseases I know. It can eat you alive at the very moment you think you look so good. When we acquire the outward trappings and the "ideal image," we often neglect the deeper issues of life—faith, character, integrity, and a desire to love God and others. We soon would rather *look* good than *be* good. In the end, the things that we acquire can turn on us and threaten our souls. In Luke 9:25, Jesus asked His disciples, "What good is it for a man to gain the whole world, and yet lose or forfeit his very self?" I like to paraphrase that verse as, "It would be really stupid if you were to live your life gaining all the things the world has to offer and then lose your life forever. If the temporary things of this world separate you from the eternal God of heaven, you'd be a fool to spend your life pursuing those things."

Like many others who wandered through the opulent '80s, I was trapped in a crossfire—the deadly battleground of my heart. Painfully and slowly, I had to learn that what I "owned" I needed to hold very loosely. That wasn't—and still isn't—an easy thing for me to do. When I hold on to something I have cherished and long felt that I needed, I often only loosen my grip one painfully pried finger at a time.

PLEASURE

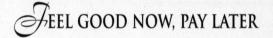

FEEL GOOD NOW, PAY LATER

Madeline's tears brought back my pain. After Sandy and I had adopted our newborn daughter, I was simply unable to listen to her cry. Every time she cried, it was like a jagged saw ripping through my heart. I would do anything to stop her crying. I suppose by the time she was three months old, I would have spoiled her beyond any hope for recovery.

My wife suggested that I seek counseling. She suspected my distress and anxiety went beyond a new parent's response to a screaming baby. No stranger by then to the benefits of wise counsel, I agreed. (Plus, I had come to learn that when Sandy makes a suggestion, it's wise to heed her advice.)

During one session, the Christian counselor and I were talking about this problem of the pain I felt when Madeline cried. He asked me to tell him my most significant memories of childhood.

"Some of my most vivid memories involve an old bathroom," I said.

I told him this with some hesitation, because if you tell a psychologist that your most vivid memories took place in a bathroom, he or she might

think, *Now we've really got something to work with!*
Needless to say, my counselor's ears perked up.

I recalled occasions early in my life when I was
in an old bathtub and the water was running. My
mother was somewhere else. I reached up and
turned off the cold water. I literally watched the
skin on my feet scald from the hot water. The
exact same horror happened exactly the same way
a short time later. It took me two times to realize
that this wasn't a good thing to do.

I also remember standing on the toilet as
someone dried me off; I slipped and my hand went
down on an old gas heater that wasn't insulated.
My whole hand became a blister. As my father
rocked me to sleep, my hand throbbed in excruci-
ating pain.

But none of those incidents was my worst
bathroom memory. The most painful time
occurred when I was about a year old. I recall
standing outside the bathroom with tears streaming
down my face as I listened to my mother crying
uncontrollably inside. I remember the deep sob-
bing sounds she made, as if her grief were so powerful that she could barely breathe. I felt the need
for help—for her and for me. I stood outside of the
door with my hands above my head, trying to turn
the doorknob.

My counselor suggested I ask my father about
what was going on in my family at that time, which

I knew was about the same time my grandfather died. When we talked, my father told me that my grandfather had not died of a heart attack as I had always been told. He had killed himself. To fight a severe depression, he had agreed to submit to electric shock therapy, which in those days ripped through the brain while the patient was wide awake. The pain and terror must have been unimaginable. He vowed never to endure that again. For a while, my grandfather was fine. Then, slowly, the depression began to overtake him again. Not wanting to face the electric shock therapy again, he chose a gun instead.

My mother wrestled with her father's death throughout my childhood. The stigma of a suicide in a Christian family was difficult for her. In addition to her deep grief, she also struggled with the same depression that prompted her father's suicide.

The memory of my mom weeping inside an old bathroom, grieving her father's suicide, was a wound that hung over my childhood. My father said it took her six years to get over it, and in some ways, I never did. That subconscious, emotional wound —and others like it that occurred throughout my childhood—I dragged into my adult life. Those wounds I was too lazy to resolve in my early life had to be confronted and left behind or I would damage my own daughter with them. It was the Christian counselor who helped me work through them. Christ freed me through that process. Now my girl's tears merely need to be dried; they do not signify for me a childhood obsessed with how to stop the pain. They have taught me well.

Feeding an Empty Ego

As a young child, I knew the truth of God's Word, at least as well as any child can. My parents taught me the tenets of the Christian faith, both in word and action. My father was actively engaged in developing and growing a church in Bryan, Texas, and my mother raised us with love, respect, and in the knowledge of the Lord. Like all parents, they were not perfect. My dad was sometimes distant and quiet; as a child, I never knew he struggled. My mom, of course, was fighting her own private battles while she tried to care for her children.

The mistakes I made were not my parents' fault. I made decisions that I knew were based on lies, or at least on the truth as I tried to reconstruct it. Because of my parents' insistence on keeping rules, I began to see God as a naysayer, a taskmaster, a great destroyer of fun and pleasure. Because I attempted so desperately to soothe the wounds of my childhood and adolescence, I had little or no concept of delayed gratification. My pain, I believed, needed immediate attention.

In seeking a quick fix, I hurt myself even more deeply. I wanted immediate pleasure. When my high school girlfriend, the light of my life, wouldn't consent to have sex, I found someone who would. Rumors followed. My girlfriend found out, and our relationship was over. I gave up a fairy-tale romance for a few moments of instant gratification. Worst of all, I hurt someone I really loved. I knew it, I felt it, and I hated the pain I had caused her. She stood for what was good, and I betrayed her with evil. I was surprised at just how deeply betrayal can hurt both the betrayed and the betrayer. That incident had a powerful impact on my life, filling me with profound regret—irreversible regret that I attempted to medicate with more sinful pleasure.

It was not just the obvious kinds of sinful plea-sures—such as sex, lewd music, drinking, and drugs—that enticed me. Pleasure, for me, became anything that fed my empty ego. For instance, I took pleasure in making my friends laugh. That's not unusual or wrong in itself, but I would go to almost any length for a big laugh. Once, after my father took his car into the shop for a buzzing noise, I retrieved it for him and drove it to the railroad tracks near our home. Five of my friends and I drove the car up on the tracks, where we revved the engine and spun the wheels until—*clank!*—it fell onto the railroad ties. We howled! (I guess you had to be there.) Slowly, we placed it back on the tracks and drove away before a train slammed into us. Before the day was over, the buzzing noise, which had been repaired, returned. My father was furious at the shop for not fixing it.

Pleasure for me was also singing a solo at church, in my best booming voice, and bringing people to tears over God's holiness. Pleasure for me was taking a handoff from the quarterback and slamming into the end zone for a winning touchdown. Pleasure for me was another award, certificate, or honor. Those things weren't bad in themselves, but my motives were.

In those early years, my search for relief brought me some degree of respect, recognition, and power. I was considered popular, well respected, and the life of the party. But I knew the truth about myself, and I was miserable. Even when I tried to earn back my self-respect, I fell deeper into sin.

In my heart of hearts, I knew the haunting truth—that I was the one who needed to change to fit the truth, instead of trying to fit my life around a lie. I knew I had become obsessed with myself, my pain, my pleasure. I knew I had bought into the lie to look out for number one and pursue a life free of pain and full of fun. As time passed, the fun became more fleeting. I even longed to return to my faith and the truth, but I had no idea how to shed the unhealthy habits I had created.

I put a good deal of energy into dreaming. I performed and I collected accomplishments like they were food for the soul. Eventually, I stacked up my successes and shaped them into a dream, which, in reality, was more like an idol. My dream was to attend college, study music, and become the greatest musician in the world. Seriously. I would stop at nothing to pursue this dream. I knew if I could just make my dream happen, I would find true pleasure.

Ironically, it was another pleasure that got in the way. In college, I dated a girl for whom I really cared. She was bright, gentle, beautiful, and energetic, as well as being a Christian. I believed we had a lot in common. Even though, in my terrible spiritual condition, I mostly judged people on external appearances, I truly had lucked out when I fell in love with her.

Because we loved each other, I had an easy time convincing her to sleep with me. I justified my sin—and hers—by believing that love covered everything. Eventually, I would discover it was less love for her and more love for myself that led me to seek sexual gratification. How shameful that I didn't see what I was doing until it was too late. She missed one period, and then she missed another. She was pregnant.

Even though I loved my girlfriend, I selfishly did not want to shatter my dream. At all costs, I had to protect the only thing I thought could save me. Never once did I consider any options. Never once did I drop down on my knees and seek God's forgiveness and ask Him to show me a responsible way out of the problem. Never once did I doubt what had to be done. She had to have an abortion.

I was deeply immersed in the philosophy of the world. If something is inconvenient—say, a broken radio, a bad marriage, or a baby—just get rid of it. So there we were, my girlfriend and I and the baby growing in her womb. I carefully laid out my plan, with all the details already put together: Go here at such and such a time, and they will do such and such to you, and then it will be over. We can both go on with our lives. I'll even pay for half of the procedure.

I never really gave her an opportunity to respond. My heartless and unbending pragmatism overwhelmed her. No unwanted baby was going to stand in the way of my musical career. So she went, because I convinced her it was the best way out of a bad situation, and because she thought I loved her.

She and I would have a 23-year-old daughter today if I had not moved to take that life away. The guilt, shame, and remorse had emotional, physical, and spiritual consequences that had such a devastating effect on me that I almost lost my life.

The Blind Leading the Blind

The summer after the abortion, I stayed with my brother Jerry in Easley, South Carolina. I killed time in a series of vacuous relationships with girls. Although I worked hard at having fun, it seemed that nothing could give me pleasure anymore. In the meantime, Jerry was having trouble of his own (which I'll discuss in the next chapter). Truly, when it came to helping one another, it was the blind leading the blind. The prodigals were headed for the pigsty.

I returned home worse than when I left. The sex, drinking, and admiration had all failed me, and the effects of the abortion began to surface. Only 20 years old, I fell into a deep depression, went on antidepressants, and began to feel as old as a grandfather. Within six months of asking my girlfriend to have an abortion, I was diagnosed with 83 ulcers. My doctor told me that I would either have to make some serious lifestyle changes or have part of my intestines or my colon removed. Within a year, I had dropped out of my music major and abandoned my dream. At the time, I had no idea what was causing me such misery. I could not recognize the negative repercussions of my behavior. The consequences of sin did, indeed, appear to me—just not as quickly as I first thought they might.

Settling for Less

I had fallen into the trap of demanding instant solutions. And why not? I lived in the world of Technology as Savior—instant banks, instant credit, instant coffee, and fast food. We pace in front of our microwaves. There is an irony here. When we demand instant fulfillment, we short-circuit the way God has made us. It is not as I believed—God was not intent on squashing all pleasure; in fact, He has wired us for intense joy. C. S. Lewis once wrote that God wants to give us pleasure, but we spend our time playing in mud puddles when He is offering us a cruise ship on the Caribbean Sea.

For instance, God created sexual passion. If He would have been interested only in propagation, He could have designed a baby button, and the husband could have turned it on at night like he might a light switch. But sex, in God's wonderful and creative design, is to be more than just a way to make babies. It is a phenomenal way of showing love and intimacy with another person. The two shall become one.

Humankind has tampered with God's plan for sexual pleasure. Outside the lifelong bond of a loving marriage, sex becomes less human. Our society has not made sex free, but has merely cheapened it. If you try to make sex "casual," "safe," and merely pleasurable, it will become destructive and demeaning. I imagine that God weeps when He sees His gift so degraded.

As Christians, we must rethink our image of God. Instead of being like the God of *Saturday Night Live*'s Church Lady, with lips puckered in prudish disdain of pleasure, our God is a progressive, fun, lover of passion and pleasure. He wants what is truly best for us. Yet at the same time, He hates it when humans experience less than what He has designed for us. He hates it when sex becomes a toy, good for a thrill or a laugh, and then is tossed away like a paper plate. He hates it when His eternal and sustaining love is sacrificed for a twin-cam Sea Ray boat or a promotion to vice president of a company. He hates it when pleasure is confused with a numbing thrill.

When we discard the truth of the Bible, we are not, like we so smugly think, throwing away an outdated, stern, irrelevant book. On the contrary, we are casting out our only real hope of deep fulfillment and lasting pleasure.

Rather than line up their behavior with Scripture, people often try to bring Scripture in line with their behavior. They write off the Bible as a book with no practical, modern application, saying, "This book is too old-fashioned" or "It was written for another day, when they just didn't understand things the way we do." To accept the truth of the Bible would be to accept the need to submit to God, and that is one thing most people are not prepared to do. As the apostle Paul writes in Romans, "They exchanged the truth of God for a lie" (1:25). And without truth, there are always consequences.

A woman recently called the counseling program I cohost. She was completely miserable. The only times in her life when she felt power and meaning were when she was in the backseat of a car with a married man. Although she hungered for those times, she knew that she was destroying herself as well as the men with whom she chose to have affairs. When the counselor asked her what she thought she could do to develop a deeper level of purpose in her life, she responded, "Help other people in some way. Do some charity work." Even though the woman was far down the path of sexual addiction, she knew instinctively that what she was doing—pursuing her own self-interests—was wrong. She was confusing real pleasure with what made her feel *good*, instead of choosing what made her feel *right*.

I understand this woman's misery. I, too, had aggravated my wounds by indulging in pleasures disconnected from God and His truth. I had created my own suffering. I can still remember the enormous emptiness and hurt I felt as I returned to school that fall after my girlfriend had the abortion. My body was wracked with ulcers, literally bleeding into itself. My mind was tormented with doubts. My soul writhed in guilt. I had no clue as to what I wanted to do with my life, and I had no one to turn to. This was where my life of pleasure-seeking had led me.

Fortunately, I came to an end of myself. In my desperation, I was able to acknowledge that I had made a complete mess of my life and that I needed God's forgiveness and strength. I found my way back to the narrow path. And even though I found God's surprising grace there, I also discovered that I had done enormous damage to myself. Because of my sin, I found the path overgrown with thorns and weeds. To this day, I still suffer some of the consequences of my sin. The roots of the world's thorn bushes and weeds grow very deep. I'm still tugging at some that refuse to be pulled up.

We all have wounds that never seem to heal— from our childhood, from our own sinful behavior, from living in the world. But the answer is not to pretend that they don't exist or believe the world's lie that we can alleviate them with self-gratifying pleasures. We must face our wounds honestly, repent before God, and let Him surprise us with His amazing and healing grace. It is only then that we can begin to experience what God has intended and desired for us all along.

CHAPTER FIVE

POWER AND CONTROL

THE SEDUCTION of SELF-SUFFICIENCY

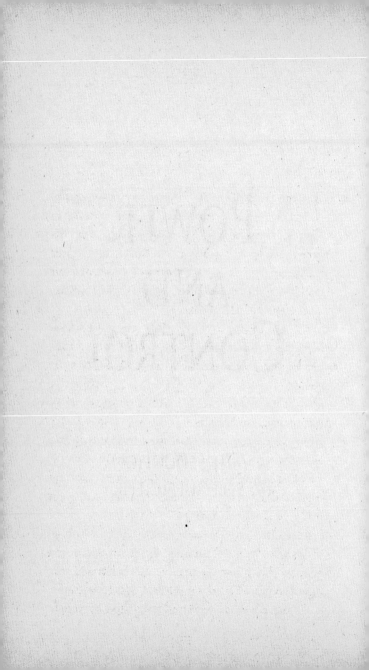

In the fall of 1984, we buried my other grandfather, my dad's dad, Art. We had gathered in Ranger, Texas, to pay our last respects. On that sunny, windy, and sad day, red dust blew around the cemetery, stinging our faces as we watched our grandfather disappear into the ground. My brother Terry delivered the eulogy.

That day, the hint of death was everywhere. My other brother Jerry was supposed to be a pallbearer, but he had come to me and said that he couldn't sustain the weight of the casket. Six months earlier, he had suffered a serious bout of pneumonia, and he still had not regained his strength. That surprised me, since Jerry was always as tough as steel, the model of vigor and resilience. I looked at him with concern and suspicion as my mind flashed back to another conversation we'd had several years before.

At that time, we were having dinner with one of his friends in a California restaurant and began arguing about homosexuality. We continued our discussion as we paid our bill and walked outside.

"The Bible has been misinterpreted by people

who condemn the gay lifestyle," Jerry protested as we faced each other in the restaurant parking lot. "It's just one of those gray areas. You can use the Bible to argue both sides of the issue."

"I disagree with you, Jerry," I told him. "I think the Bible is perfectly clear on that issue. But if you ever told me you're homosexual, you would still be my brother and I would still love you."

It was then that he first admitted to me that he was homosexual. We talked a bit more, reasonably and calmly, and then we parted. But as I drove away, my composure vanished, and I lost control.

I pounded the steering wheel and shouted, "Unbelievable! My brother—homosexual!"

I did not want to accept that my brother—a strong, popular, moral person, whom all the girls wanted to date—was homosexual.

And now, facing him at the funeral, I instinctively sensed that my brother had AIDS. A knot formed in my stomach as I realized that in just a few years, I could be attending his funeral. He must have been thinking the same thing.

∽

I really got to know Jerry during the summer after I asked my girlfriend to have an abortion. It was the summer of the Watergate trials, and the nation was disillusioned. So was I. It was an awful time in my life. Not only was I dealing with the guilt and shame over my girlfriend's abortion, I had run a stop sign and smashed into a car, causing serious damage. A couple of people received minor injuries. They had threatened to sue, which did nothing for my already-gnawing ulcers. I needed a place to escape, and my best option was Easley, South Carolina, where my brother was working as an administrator of a downtown renewal project.

Jerry put in a lot of hours at work. I put in a lot of hours with the opposite sex. From the time I arrived, I dated nearly nonstop, keeping myself so busy that I didn't have to confront the desperation I was feeling. I thought that if I just tried hard enough, I could regain some sense of control over my life.

I didn't know it at the time, but Jerry was doing no better than I was. He was also running from the hurt and insecurity in his life, trying to hide behind an image—his career, his reputation at church, and having the "right" friends. He had a knack for success. But underneath his polished exterior, his deadly secret simmered in a poisonous soup of insecurity, pain, and emptiness.

I would later learn that Jerry had been sexually abused by one of the older boys at a church camp when he was five years old. That experience, combined with having a father who was busy and often emotionally distant, formed in Jerry a powerful desire to please other men and win their approval. Most of this desire, he said, was not sexual, but a

desperate attempt to gain attention and acceptance. For the most part, he controlled his infatua-
tion with men by pretending it didn't exist. But as
that increasingly failed, he tried to cover it up with
a gold-plated image. Like me, Jerry defined himself
by exteriors.

It was during that same summer that my
brother had his first homosexual experience. After
midnight, in a swimming pool, another man locked
his legs around Jerry's waist as they hung from the
diving board. It ended there, but it was enough to
open a floodgate of emotion that swamped Jerry's
carefully constructed defenses. I should have
noticed his confusion and distress, but I, too, was
drowning in a pool of pain.

Creating Ourselves in Our Own Image

Shirley MacLaine, the guru of New Age channeling, says that each of us has the power to be a god.
What's more, she says that each of us *is* God. The
only problem is, MacLaine contends, some of us
don't know that we're God. So once we know
we're God and start acting like Him, then we will
find the fulfillment of being God.

Like Adam and Eve in the Garden, we are all
tempted to believe this Grand Lie. We all want to
be like God, to control our own destinies. With this
subtle form of idolatry, we place our own goals and
aspirations above God, which in turn suppresses

God's ability to guide us and use us as He chooses. Let me be clear: I am not saying that all of our plans and goals are selfish attempts to grab power for ourselves. After all, God gave each of us brains to use and gifts to employ as we strive to make our time on earth count for something. But we must submit our desires and aspirations to God and be ready to alter our course according to His will and leading. As Proverbs 16:3 says, "Commit to the Lord whatever you do, and your plans will succeed." When we forget about God in the pursuit of our own whims, we risk making our endeavors into idols. I love the imagery of Psalm 115:4–8, which speaks of the consequences of constructing idols in our lives:

> *But their idols are silver and gold, made by the hands of men. They have mouths, but cannot speak, eyes, but they cannot see; they have ears, but cannot hear, noses, but they cannot smell; they have hands, but cannot feel, feet, but they cannot walk; nor can they utter a sound with their throats. Those who make them will be like them, and so will all who trust in them.*

Of course, you and I are too sophisticated and progressive to worship statues fashioned of gold, bronze, or wood. That would be too blatant, too flagrant. So we ever-so-subtly shift ourselves to center stage, putting our desires and goals into the spotlight and ahead of everything else. We begin to create ourselves in our own image. In a sense, we make ourselves a god.

Some people are better than others at creating good-looking images. Since an image depends upon external comparison, there will always be some haves and some have-nots. And in the tension between those with and those without comes strife, conflict, and opposition—sometimes even violence and destruction.

Over the past decade we have seen wars and massacres in places such as Haiti, Rwanda, and Bosnia. Atrocities have occurred there and in hundreds of other places in the world because some people are power-hungry. They want influence and position for themselves, and they are willing to hurt anyone to achieve it. For them, the good life is something for which to kill.

Other battles for power and control are far more subtle. Perhaps it is a ladder-climber at the office who tramples on a coworker's good name to get a promotion and the corner office. Or maybe it is a president of a large organization who uses fear and intimidation to maximize his employees' productivity and build his empire. Or perhaps it is a psychologist, climbing on a pile of degrees, slinging psychobabble to defend his unethical position. Or maybe it is a Christian woman, firmly self-right-eous, who *knows* she could run the outreach pro-gram better than the current leader—and lets everybody know it.

We often hoard power, position, time, and prestige, thinking that if we gather enough, we will finally feel better about ourselves. But there is a serious catch to this plan: We can never obtain enough power or control to make our idols, our images, live. They are dead, worthless, hollow. They have not even a hint of life.

In a sudden twist, Psalm 115:8 warns us, "Those who make them will be like them, and so will all who trust in them." With a psychological and spiri-tual insight second to none, the Bible states that the idols we create—those lifeless, external objects of worship—will not only fail to deliver, but they will actually kill us in the process. By trying to take total control of our lives, we do damage to our souls.

When control becomes our mode of thinking and acting, we will sooner or later begin to treat people like things. When I realized I was doing this with people on our New Life Clinics staff, it was quite a shock. I, a great lover of people, had become a user of people. I had to get away, breach the pattern, and restore the love I had lost.

Many parents control their children in one way or another—some are strict disciplinarians who care more about how their children appear to others than they do about developing genuine character. Some parents, having had their own dreams dashed, live vicariously through their children, pushing them to excel in gymnastics or music against the wishes of their kids.

Control often occurs in marriage, too. What about the husband who tries to control his wife? He may quote Scripture at her, but he actually wants her to become submissive or more like him so he will like her better. Instead of creating the loving environment necessary for her to fulfill her God-given potential, he demands that she change and see things his way. He fashions an idol in the distorted image of his own self.

In my life, I had to hit bottom before I could admit that I was ignoring God and trying to control my own destiny. I realized that I could not play the game anymore. No matter how hard I tried, I could no longer work up the energy or the desire to continue on the path that had brought me so much pain. For once, I could not act or perform my way out of a situation. The only real option was to confess my sin before God and rely on His sustaining grace as I walked painfully through the consequences of my mistakes.

Grabbing Control vs. Refusing Responsibility

Our society encourages us to focus on ourselves. We prize individualism and autonomy, often at the expense of community and cooperation. We love the loners, the John Waynes and Clint Eastwoods, who follow their own rules and don't take guff from anyone. Advertisements tell us to indulge ourselves, because "you deserve it." The courts focus on individual rights, and as a result, our country and communities have suffered deep divisions. As individuals, we believe it is our "right" to pursue happiness.

The need for control is a disease with many symptoms. It can be quite blatant and aggressive. I recently heard a tape by G. Gordon Liddy, who was part of the Nixon Administration during Watergate and is now a successful talk show host. Most of his life story is a testimony to the power of self. In his book *Will*, he describes how he would go to almost any length to keep control over his life. His particular lifelong battle was with fear.

Rather than run from fear, Liddy stared it down. To conquer his fear of electricity, for example, Liddy crawled up a telephone pole until he was so close to the high-intensity wire that his hair stood on end. But Liddy held on, and afterward he was no longer afraid of electricity. Another time, to conquer his fear of rats, he captured one, killed it, and cooked its haunches for his lunch. He never feared rats again. Liddy was committed to the theory of control. He was the ultimate in tough-guy, I-don't-need-anyone self-sufficiency. Even after his arrest and imprisonment for masterminding the Watergate break-in, he remained firm in his resolve, in the power of his own will.

Once, Chuck Colson, a fellow conspirator in the cover-up and then a new Christian, approached Liddy in his jail cell. He asked, "Mr. Liddy, have you seen the light?"

"Mr. Colson," Liddy replied, "I'm not even looking for the switch."

In contrast to Liddy's aggressive pursuit of control, others take a defensive approach. Instead of overcoming, they allow themselves to be overcome. At no other point in our country's history has there been such an epidemic of "victims"—people who have declared themselves powerless against their circumstances, genes, metabolism, or upbringing. Rather than seeing his vulnerability and protecting himself, the alcoholic says, "Drinking problems run in my family—it's genetic. There's nothing I can do about it." The criminal says, "It's not my fault that I steal. I had lousy parents who didn't teach me any better." Our culture hands out excuses like ATM machines dispense cash.

I am not saying that our circumstances, genes, and upbringing do not affect who we are. But we are responsible for our own behavior. With the help of God, all of us are capable of change. Sometimes people allow their lives to self-destruct simply so they can play the helpless role of victim or martyr.

I frequently see people who create or allow circumstances to develop that destroy them. Some people accumulate heavy debt, or flounder in a bad job, or refuse to resolve bad relationships. Instead of taking responsibility for their lives, they allow them to crumble and then fall back on excuses, such as bad luck, bad genes, or bad parents. Christians will often find an excuse to ask God for a miracle, or to raise an angry, clenched fist at Him. The power in such victim mentality is that we never have to blame ourselves. It is always someone else's fault—our boss, our God, our friends, the Tri-Lateral Commission, the liberal Democrats. The problems are anybody's fault but our own.

My brother Jerry fell into this trap. Wrestling with his homosexual behavior, he became angry at God for "giving him" homosexual feelings. He prayed diligently and fervently for God to take away the feelings. Yet, at the same time, he did little to remove himself from circumstances that might prompt those same feelings. In essence, he wanted change without facing the pain that comes with it. Jerry tried the best he knew how. On more than one occasion, he tried to escape the homosexual world; once, he even lasted a year. But he would always return when the pain became too great. He craved the attention and acceptance the gay lifestyle offered and was unwilling to honestly face the deeper issues in his life. Jerry was sincere, but he lacked the accountability and understanding to make his commitment stick. He discovered that you can't leave one way of life unless you enter into another one full of support and healthy relationships.

Finally, Jerry's choices caught up with him. In April 1985, while hospitalized with a bout of pneumonia, he was diagnosed with AIDS. The suspicions I'd had at my grandfather's funeral were confirmed. Jerry tried to live in secrecy for a year and a half, but eventually he was forced to disclose his condition or face death alone. His first step was to acknowledge his homosexuality as sin. In his book, *How Will I Tell My Mother?* he writes, "What does come from it [homosexuality] is a complete destruction of mind, body, spirit, and the inability to utilize God-given talents to accomplish great things for His glory." While he was specifically referring to homosexuality, his description certainly applies to sin in general.

After repenting of his wrongdoing, Jerry sought our family's forgiveness, which was extended to him in unconditional love. He then determined to make the rest of his life count for God, no matter how long that might be. He wrote, "I told God that He had my body, mind, and soul. I was done, and I was played out." He entered counseling to begin to understand the underlying issues in his life and, as he was freed from his self, he began to serve others. He ministered to people dying of AIDS in hospitals and care facilities, many of whom had been abandoned by family and friends. Though he was gaunt, crippled, and nearly breathless from the ravaging disease, Jerry finally felt a deep sense of wholeness in his soul.

⬥

It was supposed to be a joke. G. Gordon Liddy, appearing on David Letterman's show, tossed off the comment as casually as a fisherman tosses old bait. In response to the question, "What happens when you die?" Liddy responded, "Worm meat. Eventually the coffin disintegrates in the ground, and you become food for worms. That is where it all ends."

For years, this punch line soured in Liddy's soul. There had to be a difference between funny and tragic. A purposeless life was tragic, not funny. Finally, Liddy, the king of self-sufficiency, surrendered control of his life to God. "Not my will," he prayed, "but Your will." God surprised even the strongest of wills. I don't know where Mr. Liddy is today in his walk with God. What I do know is that a man with an unusually strong will came face-to-face with himself and surrendered—like my dying brother did—to the power and control of the Creator.

⬥

On June 13, 1988—almost three years after his diagnosis—Jerry Arterburn died due to complications of the AIDS virus. His funeral, while not without grief, was a celebration. He died feeling the joy that comes when we relinquish control of our lives to God. Those who attended the funeral were struck by the contrast between what we do to ourselves when we take control and what God can do when we surrender to His power.

CHAPTER SIX

COMFORT

Hindering growth *by* avoiding pain

It seems that we live in a time when everybody wants a miracle. We want a miracle to fix our finances; a miracle to fix our marriage; a miracle for instant healing. Some people who crave a miracle aren't even particularly religious, unless you can count the god of technology or the universal god of pure white light among your list of qualified saviors. If we do happen to believe in the real God, we sometimes have Him bustling around the cosmos with our own personal shopping lists.

But today's mind-set is about more than just wanting a miracle or two. We want it now—and without any inconvenience on our part. We expect God to clean up after us, prevent us from suffering the consequences of our own behavior, or remove the reality of pain and struggle from this world. It's like God should serve up miracles like pizzas, as long as we throw Him a tip now and then.

Hiding behind the paper-thin walls we have managed to build with our own puny hands—our odd collection of things, titles, and accomplishments—we pretend that the world is somehow not so evil. We believe we are safe. And then when disaster strikes and the fire devours our walls in an instant, we are left shopping for miracles. When one doesn't appear, we burn in anger at God.

What most people really desire is not so much comfort as an absence of pain. Those intent on avoiding pain rarely take risks, which are always necessary for joy. They no longer look outside the boundaries of their own walls, because they haven't always liked what they have seen. They have confused distraction with occasional glimpses of happiness.

People will go to unbelievable lengths to avoid pain and discomfort—in marriage, parenting, work, and almost every area of life. Instead of dealing with problems head-on, which might spark conflict, they pretend the problems don't exist or they divert their energies elsewhere—sex, chocolate, work, football, shopping, TV—and often create a fairly convincing image of security and peace. But the security is false, and the peace is costly.

The problem with trying to avoid pain is that it can't be done for very long. As much as this world is filled with beauty and grace, it is also saturated with evil and pain. The question should not be "How can I avoid pain?" but "How can I best deal with it when it comes?" The underlying terror for people who live in the comfort zone is not in any external threat but in their helplessness to deal with pain when it comes. By avoiding the harsh realities of life, they cut themselves off from internal development.

A life based on avoiding pain requires a complex and interrelated foundation of lies. At nearly every level of existence, the reality of life is denied. And, as we saw in chapter 2, when a person lives any part of his life based on a lie, he is bound for eventual trouble. The terrible irony for a person who pursues only comfort is that, in the end, he will have more trouble and pain than he knows what to do with.

The Nature of the World

People who live in the comfort zone believe (or act as if they do) that they are entitled to happiness and they can secure it on their own. *Sure*, they think, *there are things that go wrong, but if I just keep looking, I can find fulfillment in this world.* This could be called the grass-is-greener-on-the-other-side philosophy. If a marriage doesn't work, get a divorce and find "the right person." If a job is giving you trouble, quit and find "the right one." If a friend makes you mad, find "a new one." If your church isn't meeting your needs, find "a better one." Much of this thinking, although as ancient as Rome, has been fueled in our culture by the savior of technology. It has promised a new world, one filled with convenience, pleasure, infinite gadgetry, and everything "new and improved." If you don't like something, just wait a few moments and its enhanced replacement will be available.

People who buy into this view of the world spend their lives banking on the future, waiting for the next gadget, the next promotion, the next marriage. Eventually, the thinking goes, the right one or the right thing will come along, and it will bring bliss.

Some of our churches, I'm afraid, feed the lie of this world. By focusing on God as the potential source of the greatest new-and-improved life, teachers and preachers sometimes fail to provide a realistic picture of the world's pain, evil, sin, and persecution of Christians. One pastor I know, who is genuinely struggling for a better balance, put it this way: "When do we tell them about the lions?"

The Nature of Self

A foundation of ignorance underlies the attitude that life is a pain-free joy ride. In the pursuit of the new and improved, we assume that change—at least on our part—is not really necessary. The problem is not with me—say, a flawed character or a broken soul or a short temper—but with other people or the circumstances. The problem is that I am a possessor of these *rights*, and they have not been fulfilled. I am basically a good person with some bad luck.

Pain reminds people in the comfort zone that all is not right. Guilt and shame, which are often consequences of sin, turn the pointing finger in the wrong direction. It is amazing to what lengths people will go to make the finger point in some other direction, to assure themselves that the blame lies elsewhere. Often, such people choose to surround themselves with others to whom they feel superior. A high school girl, wrestling with poor self-esteem, will often surround herself with delinquents or underachievers so she can feel better. *See, I'm not so bad. Look at them.* The problem is that the people she has surrounded herself with will almost certainly further lower her self-esteem.

This is true on a spiritual level as well. How many times have you heard someone describe himself as "basically good," or at least not a terrible person. "I'm no Hitler," he might say. "Now *he* was evil." Because it improperly moves evil outside the realm of self, this attitude denies reality at the deepest level. In his book *The Spirit of the Disciplines*, Dallas Willard writes about this deadly deception:

> *[It] signals a lack of insight—willing or unwilling—into the forces that inhabit the normal human personality and thereby move or condition the usual course of human events. Above all, it*

*shows a failure to understand that the
immediate support of evils universally
deplored lies in the simple readiness of
"decent individuals" to harm others or
allow harm to come to others when the
conditions are "right." That readiness
comes into play whenever it will help us
realize our goals of security, ego gratification, or satisfaction of bodily desires. This
systematic readiness that pervades the
personality of normal, decent human
beings is fallen human nature.*[1]

Admitting that there is sin in my life is to
acknowledge that the evil in the world is, to some
degree, my responsibility. That, of course, is an
extremely painful admission. Even more painful is
the corresponding realization that change is necessary—not in external circumstances or relationships,
but within myself, at the deepest levels of my being.
Eventually the admission of sin leads to the loss of
self-control, for where there is sin, there is a need for
a sinless savior. For a person in the comfort zone,
helplessness is the worst kind of pain.

The Nature of God

The Bible says "it is a dreadful thing to fall into the
hands of the living God" (Hebrews 10:31). God, in
His holiness, cannot tolerate sin—He burns it as

surely and completely as a moth in flame. It is painful to believe in a holy God who cannot tolerate our destructive behavior. To believe in a God who hates sin requires an admission of our insufficiency and His complete sovereignty. Since only God can atone for sin—through the substitutionary death of His Son, Jesus—we are left to His complete mercy.

Let us be honest: Most of us chafe at the idea that we are dependent upon someone else; it is uncomfortable to realize that we are not sufficient. So to run from the painful reality of our complete need for God, we reinvent Him. In this way, we are not created in His image, but He becomes created in *our* image. I love the verse in Psalms in which God says, "You thought I was altogether like you" (50:21). It is not surprising, then, that our culture conjures up all kinds of soft, comfortable notions of God—the warm, white light, the universal oneness, the god in all of us. We humans know that we are spiritual, but we prefer our exposure to the supernatural in kindly doses.

But when we reduce God to a big lie in the form of a human size, we doom ourselves to a reality no greater than ourselves. We are trapped in sin, focused on the self, without real hope in this world or another one to come. Cut off from the source of love and life, we pretend not to notice that even the best that we do is somehow sorely lacking.

Without the true God, we have no hope of a full life. But with the true God, we face the greater pain of submission, repentance, and change. We choose, more times than not, to live without God, simply because we do not want to face the discomfort of altering our behavior and acknowledging that we desperately need help.

The Nature of Change

Growth and development require honesty, and honesty is often painful. This is where many people get stuck. They are simply unwilling to endure the discomfort necessary to grow emotionally and spiritually, so they stay mired in their current harmful situation. When we refuse to painfully resolve issues in our lives, we are, in effect, giving them more power. And instead of having control over our lives, which is what we sought in the first place, we become controlled. An unresolved issue in your life will stay buried for only so long before it shows up in some destructive way. It's like the rattle you hear under the hood of your car—you can pretend it's not there, but sooner or later, you'll be forced to deal with it (probably after you break down on the highway).

Recently, an angry man called the radio counseling program that I cohost.

"I just beat the tar out of my fiancée, and I need some help," he said.

My colleague, Dave Stoop, and I began to explore the sources of this man's anger. We were looking for the people in his past he had not forgiven, people who had formed the root of bitterness that resulted in his outbursts of rage.

"Where do you think all this anger came from?" I asked. "Was there something in your childhood that had a dramatic effect on your life?"

He thought for a while and said, "Well, when I was a young boy, about five years old, there were several men who molested me. These men belonged to our church."

"Where was your father during this time?" Dave asked. "Why didn't your dad protect you from these men?"

"My father and I didn't have much of a relationship," the man explained. "He was very distant. While all of this was happening, he wasn't around. He had abandoned our family. He's dead now."

I asked, "How do you feel about those men?"

"I've forgiven them."

I continued, "And what about your dad? How do you feel about him?"

Instantly, this man responded, "Oh, I love him very much."

Then I paused and said, "You must be a Christian."

"Yeah, why do you ask?"

"Because you are saying all the right things," I

explained, "but your life doesn't make one bit of sense. For men who molested you, you use the word forgiveness. And for a father who abandoned you, you use the word love. But you admitted a few moments ago that you beat the tar out of the person you have chosen to spend the rest of your life with."

This man had refused to painfully resolve what happened to him as a child, and as a result, the abuse and the abandonment controlled his adult life. What he needed to do was grieve his lost childhood and work through the trauma he had experienced. He also needed to admit that his feelings for his father were nothing close to love. Painfully and honestly, he needed to resolve his anger, come to a place of real forgiveness, and release the problem. He had grown comfortable with his angry feelings and had learned to cover them up with the words Christians use, such as *love* and *forgiveness*. This man exemplified someone who had carried a problem that he didn't cause but only he could resolve. Until he was willing to do that, the problem would continue to adversely affect all of his relationships.

When we choose to confront problems in our lives—no matter how painful and uncomfortable—God is able to bring healing to our hearts and souls. And He can then use the problems that inflicted pain to become a source of comfort and hope for others. As we remove some of the most corrosive substances in our souls—such as bitterness, resentment, and anger—God is able to use us in a new way.

The nature of true change demands the truth. When we lie to ourselves about the pain of the world, self, God, and relationships, we cut ourselves off from any hope of lasting and real change. The world has it wrong. Change is never easy, certainly not as easy as licking a stamp and sending off for a new-and-improved soul from the L.L. Bean catalog. To become genuinely new and improved, you have to deal with the old and worthless. And that, in almost every case, will involve a good deal of pain. When we choose this route, however, God surprises us and meets us at the point of our greatest despair and pain with His comfort and grace.

The Nature of Grace

Christians are the recipients of God's grace, but let's not confuse grace with an easy excuse to do whatever we want. Grace allows us to grow into Him, and as we do so, we will experience life fully. To be thoroughly alive and one with Christ and His body—the church—we must sacrifice, relinquish our me-first attitudes, and give up all of our hidden sins. God gives us the environment of His grace— His unconditional love—so we can learn to be fully human, to develop and use the gifts that He has given us. His love is there so we can take painful chances and fail, all the while knowing that we are still loved. As we yield and submit to God's will, His Spirit will transform us into something we thought was impossible.

Dave was an all-American guy. He starred in football at California State University. He was a Christian who loved God and served Him. He volunteered in prisons, telling convicts about the good news of the gospel. Once, while he was hugging a mass murderer just before the man's execution, a painful thought hit Dave: *I am showing more love to this condemned killer than I am to my own father.*

God had convinced him of his need to forgive his father. But this was a painful thing for Dave to do. Up until age 14, Dave had wet the bed. He did so almost every time he heard his father pull into the driveway, because his father, for no other reason than that he was drunk, would often come to his room and beat him.

One night, Dave sat in the dining room when his father approached him and began beating him violently. Dave had forgotten to take out the trash. All of a sudden, Dave felt a burning sensation on his back. He turned his head to see blood and his father stabbing him with the sharp end of a bottle opener. Dave quickly gathered his younger brother and sister and went away from home to a safe spot. Together, they plotted to kill their father. When the three siblings returned to the house, they could not believe what they saw through their living room window. Their dad was cheerfully dancing with their mom as if nothing had happened. As Dave's parents danced, the confusion in his head worsened and the wounds in his heart deepened. Over the years, these wounds festered into a strong hatred of his father.

But years later in that prison, Dave felt the unmistakable call from God to forgive his father. And so, after processing and understanding his feelings about his traumatic upbringing, he decided to talk to his dad. He walked onto the family farm and trudged into the middle of a field where his dad was working. He got down on his knees and said, "Dad, I've harbored bad feelings against you for a long time. I've hated you for the way you treated me. I want you to forgive me. I've never thanked you for giving me life. I never thanked you for being my father."

Dave went on to explain to his dad that because he was given life, he was able to develop a relationship with God's Son, Jesus Christ. He had experienced God's grace, and he wanted to respond in kind to his dad. The father fell down on his knees and, to the best of his ability, prayed: "God, if Your Son is anything like my son, I want Him in my life." That night, he became a Christian. Now Dave and his dad have a restored relationship. Of course, they had a lot of painful experiences to address and work through, but they both chose the uncomfortable path in order to find healing and wholeness.

Clearly, not all of our situations will work out so cleanly. God created people with free wills, and there is always choice. But my point is this: When we choose to painfully face difficult issues, there is no telling how God will surprise us. Always, He will help to develop us into the people He wants us to be and give us the gift of a transformed, new-and-improved soul.

It is easy to become too comfortable. But we must trust God to help us face what is not pleasant, what causes pain. As we grow, we come to realize that avoiding pain now intensifies its severity later. It is a surprise to many that God is not always a God of comfort. It is an even greater surprise that we will never know Him fully unless we meet Him as we face pain, endure it, and grow from it. What a surprise. That which we seek to avoid is the very thing that would lead us into the arms of God.

Are you comfortable? How about allowing God to help you become dissatisfied with a comfortable life?

CHAPTER SEVEN

OUR WOUNDS

THE CONSEQUENCES of BAD DECISIONS

Growing up, much of my life revolved around television. My grandfather was the first person in our town to own a color TV. I clearly remember the day it arrived; it cast a spell on everyone who gathered around it in his living room. Our family's set was not as modern as my grandfather's—it was an old black-and-white unit that took about a minute for the dot in the center of the screen to disappear after the set was turned off. I recall that because when our parents pulled in the driveway, we hoped the dot would fade before they came in the house, catching us with the TV on instead of doing homework or chores.

What I liked best about television were those early game shows. For a while, I was fascinated by game show hosts—their snazzy clothes, smooth talk, and control over all the proceedings. Later, I became intrigued by the television preachers, most of whom did *not* know how to dress, with their garish and shiny suits, which matched their silver tongues.

I sometimes wondered what would happen if game show hosts and TV preachers could be combined. I could imagine the sermon: "Behind door number one is earthly pleasure. Behind door number two is eternal salvation. And behind door number three is atheism." The contestants would pick a door and then, before their eyes, the curtain would rise and they would immediately see the result of their choice. Some would be assumed to glory, while others . . . well, let's just say they would get the consolation prize (some consolation!).

Television preachers and game show hosts provided a strange foundation for my life. One show, *Truth or Consequences*, particularly caught my attention. From 1940 to 1957, Ralph Edwards hosted it on radio, then it went to TV, where Bob Barker became the host. To win cash prizes, contestants had to tell the truth to various questions or pay the consequences, which ranged from having molasses poured on their laps to being forced to wash an elephant.

The show worked well on television because of its immediacy. The action—either the truth or the consequence—unfolded right before everyone's eyes. You never had to wait until the following week to see what would happen. In one sense, the show was like life, because consequences must be paid if you don't act according to truth. But in another sense, it distorted reality in that the consequences were always immediate.

The concept of that game show has stuck with

me through much of my life. I have always wanted the consequences, either good or bad, to be immediate. In my early childhood, I tested God by departing from the truth and, when the earth didn't swallow me, I decided that breaking the rules wasn't so bad after all. On the flip side, I believed God would save me before I sank so deeply into sin that I would have to suffer consequences. I was wrong on both counts.

What I realized was that the consequences of my behavior weren't immediate. Unlike the world of television, where stories or contests unfold in minutes, the consequences of my actions took years to reveal themselves. In fact, the path of self-fulfillment was at times even pleasant and exciting. There were just enough tastes of happiness to keep me going down the wrong paths. Even well after the consequences began to appear—in the form of deep guilt, disappointment, someone's hurt feelings—I continued down the wrong road. I did so mainly because I was proud and confused: too proud to admit my mistakes, and too confused to understand that my choices were affecting me spiritually, emotionally, and psychologically.

When Truth Is Discarded

In the "free-thinking" culture of the '60s, our society, to a large extent, abandoned the truth of God's words. Using the language of freedom and love, the hippies and flower children asserted that they were no longer going to follow the rules. They promoted sex outside of marriage, drug use for pleasure, and love without commitment. They tried to free us all from outdated traditions and rules. They sought peace, love, and harmony. And for a while, it seemed to work. The Vietnam War ended. Civil Rights sprouted in the name of equality. There were some good things that came out of that rebellious and defiant decade.

But there was a big problem. In their pursuit, these "liberators" forgot that freedom is not really freedom unless it is connected with truth. If you are in jail and tell yourself you're free, you still have to find a key to unlock the cell. If you tell yourself that sex is free, the lie may last a while, but the price will be paid sooner or later. By discarding the truth of God's Word, the generation of the '60s sent us into a tailspin of deadly consequences, some of which are just now appearing in our culture. The '60s were followed by the confusing '70s, the greedy '80s, and the desperate '90s. To see the consequences of a culture that has turned its back on God, you need look no farther than the daily newspaper or TV news. The mind-numbing crimes and statistics reported there show the loss of moral direction that results from a vacuum of truth.

Without truth, man naturally slips into his fallen, sinful nature. The law of God—to serve others in love—is replaced by the law of the jungle—to look out for number one. Man's law dictates: Watch your back. You can't please everyone, so you might as well please yourself. If it feels good, do it. These were all the natural and deformed offspring of a movement spawned in the '60s, which discarded God and truth as irrelevant. Now, several decades later, the results are in: Self-fulfillment doesn't work. Yet despite its failure, many people still refuse to return to the truth.

Sin Is Toxic

We seem to have given ourselves over to the philosophy of the bumper sticker that says (I'll paraphrase), "Evil Happens." In other words, evil just is. Bad things happen and there's nothing we can do about it.

These days, a mention of sin is good for a giggle. It's a dusty concept for the uninitiated, the unenlightened, or the simply uncool. Now, responsibility is seldom personal. Because evil *just happens*, cause-and-effect has lost its relevance. And it is not just non-Christians who have allowed the reality of sin to fade into a useless metaphor. Many Christians have also lost respect for its power. If the world giggles at sin, then the church smirks. By the blood of Jesus, we say, our sin is covered. But this admission often reduces the level of sin's power to the breath required to say, "Father, forgive me." The victory over darkness may be won, but the world still spins out of control . . . and so do many believers right along with it.

The Bible does no such injustice to sin. It is clear that sin has enormously destructive power: "For the wages of sin is death" (Romans 6:23). Sin kills everything that it touches: relationships, trust, hope, faith, love, and finally, the physical body. Sin killed Jesus.

Part of the problem with sin is its invisibility. After all, most sin is unseen. When someone cheats, for example, the wrongdoing disappears into thin air, so there is a tendency to believe that the damage is only temporary. We easily lose track of sin.

I think of sin as pollution. And perhaps the greatest recent example of "visible" pollution was the oil fires started during the Persian Gulf War. In a cover story of *Time* magazine, an essayist wrote, "The oil fires over Kuwait would be evil made visible."[1] I believe the similarities between the fires and sin go much farther.

During that war, more than 600 "wild" wells were on fire. Each fire burned at a temperature of 4,000 degrees, turning nearby sand into liquid glass. As oil gushed from the well at a force of 5,000 pounds per square inch, flames rose to 400 feet and smoke billowed as high as two miles into the sky.

What happened when more than five million barrels of crude oil—worth about $87 million a day or $1,000 a second—went up in thick, black smoke each day? Day turned into night, soot fell like black snowflakes, rain became greasy and charcoal gray, car windows streaked black in a drizzle, and the air was heavy and suffocating. The picture, even at a casual glance, provides an illustration for sin. "It feels like someone is standing on your chest all the time," said one resident of Kuwait.

The Old Testament prophet Ezekiel wrote of a similar feeling of suffocation: "Our offenses and sins weigh us down, and we are wasting away because of them" (33:10). What would we see if sin became visible? Wouldn't its effects be much the same as that of hundreds of oil fires? Isn't this a dramatic picture of selfishness? Billions of consuming fires—each representing the needs, desires, and greed of individuals—spewing black plumes that darken the horizon.

It gets worse. The smoke from the oil wells turned out to be toxic. "There is a real danger to human life," said one Western diplomat. The byproducts of the combustion—including 50,000 tons a day of sulfur dioxide, the primary component of acid rain—were poisonous. But here's the *really* bad news. The effects don't go away. Long after the fires had been extinguished and the smoke clouds had dissipated, toxins continued to spread. Carried by the wind, dropped by the rain, absorbed in the soil, and running with the rivers, the poison saturates the area. It gets into the food chain. It disappears and goes underground. Who knows when and to what degree it will reappear in the form of illness, a tumor, or a deformity? No one is exempt, not even the innocent. "I think the whole region is in for a bath of carcinogenic, mutagenic, and possibly teratogenic chemicals," said one environmentalist.

Sin is like that. A lie, for example, never disappears. The liar's son grows up watching his father lie and consequently is taught the value of lying. Then the son lies and dissolves the trust in his own relationships, creating a pattern. There is no such thing as isolated sin. It wounds others. And these victims, in their attempt to handle the pain, may turn to destructive solutions, which temporarily numb the pain but end up causing more damage. The deadly cycle becomes unleashed from one person to the next, one generation to the next. Sin is enormously destructive and cyclical.

I had lunch with a man whose father was an alcoholic. It was amazing to me how far-reaching the deadly effects of sin were in his life. This man's brother was an alcoholic in his second marriage to a woman who was dying from anorexia and weighed only 80 pounds. Of their three sons, two had already been through drug rehabilitation. A third son never made it to rehab because three days before our lunch, he died of a drug overdose—the son of a son settling for the same suicidal hand-me-downs. Sin not only breeds sin, but it also attracts it. Wounded and hurting people attract wounded and hurting people—who often wound and hurt one another. The Bible says of the overwhelming power of sin: "The Lord is slow to anger, abounding in love and forgiving sin and rebellion. Yet he does not leave the guilty unpunished; he punishes the children for the sin of the fathers to the third and fourth generation" (Numbers 14:18).

The wounds of sin surround us. We live in a culture committed to feeling good rather than being right. Within each of us is a tremendous capacity to sin—to feed the self and starve others around us. We are left, it seems, with a deep sense of hopelessness. Even so great a man as the apostle Paul cried out from the dilemma, "What a wretched man I am! Who will rescue me from this body of death?" (Romans 7:24).

But there is good news. Where sin is, there is the possibility of even more grace. In fact, Paul answers his own plea by saying, "Thanks be to God—through Jesus Christ our Lord!" (Romans 7:25). In the hopelessness and desperation of sin, God can surprise us with His amazing, transforming, and powerful love. I know. I have been at the lowest point and have seen God remarkably transfer my greatest weaknesses and my worst sins into strengths and tools for service. Where once I told my girlfriend to have an abortion, I now have the opportunity to speak to thousands of people about the pain of such a choice. Where once I despaired over the lack of direction in my life, I now have been graciously given a ministry that counsels thousands of people across the country. Believe me, I am not boasting. I know exactly where I would be if not for the grace of God.

I have also seen God work in the lives of others. My mom, for instance, could have easily succumbed to the same forces of passed-down sin that drove her father to suicide. Her genes, as well as mine, have the same predisposition to depression. But unlike my grandfather, my mother and I have accepted the truth: Life is going to be a little more difficult for us, but depression is part of who we are. Acknowledging this, we are much more dependent upon the power of God to sustain us. Holding on to God's grace, we refuse to let destructive actions pass into another generation and damage the ones we love the most.

The real surprise, I suppose, is the way God takes us beyond mere survival. He transforms difficult, damaging experiences into powerful assets. After losing her son to AIDS, my mother could have easily given in to depression and helplessness. But my mother trusted in God. It wasn't that she didn't grieve the loss of her son and the sense of wasted potential, but she grieved without losing sight of God's grace. And God not only protected her, but He also transformed her sorrow into purpose. She became a living example of Psalm 126:5–6: "Those who sow in tears will reap with songs of joy. He who goes out weeping, carrying seed to sow, will return with songs of joy, carrying sheaves with him." To this day, my mother visits prisons and hospitals, taking a videotape that Jerry made before his death. She knows the deep joy that comes from ministering to those who are hurting and dying.

There's no doubt that sin wounds. Jesus Christ, on the cross, received nails through His hands and feet, a lance in His side, and fatal wounds in His soul. Sinless, He accepted the wounds and pain of all of our sins. He is the source of our hope. Our wounds can become His wounds.

A SOUL RESTORED

PART TWO

THE PATH LESS CHOSEN

ONE WAY *to* RESTORATION

I remember the trip like it was yesterday. It was October of 1973, and I was in my car driving home from a Bill Gothard seminar. My parents had signed me up, and I was so desperate to find solutions to my messed-up life that I agreed to attend. Strange things had been going on in my heart, rumblings that I had not known for a long time. In one sense, I was giving up some things; in another sense, I was being stripped of them. At the seminar, I had made a list of all the people I had hurt through my sins—my reckless self-seeking—in order to write to them or call them later to ask their forgiveness. It was an incredibly painful act that provided an unexpected and enormous sense of relief.

In the car, I grabbed a pack of cigarettes and shredded them. I remember my violence spread tobacco over the car like a pod of seeds cast by a strong wind. I had wanted to quit not only smoking, but all of the self-destructive habits I had adopted. I was exhausted, broken, and desperate enough to believe that I could begin again. In the darkness, I prayed, *Help, Lord. Give me a second chance.* That was the gist of it. I was determined to trust in God and not myself.

As I drove, I felt an overwhelming sense of forgiveness, of relief, hope, and euphoria all at once. Never before or after have I felt so overwhelmed by God. The Lord's presence was so strong that He might have been sitting in the passenger seat of my Oldsmobile. For the first time in my life, I truly gave control over to God. Even though I didn't have a clue of what the future held, I was less anxious than at any other time. I was certain of nothing but this: God had my life and soul in His hands, and He loved me.

What a strange ride. With tobacco strewn throughout the car, my dreams scattered, my body riddled with ulcers, and without a clue of where I was headed, I experienced perfect peace. Struck with flashes of understanding, I marveled at the sense of freedom I could have by simply trusting in God. I realized for the first time that I didn't have to manipulate and manufacture to make my life happen. As I gave control of my life over to God, truly trusting in His loving promises to meet my needs, I experienced a profound sense of security that comes only from complete surrender.

The sense of emptiness vanished. I understood that my mad searches for power, position, and prestige—attempts to control my own destiny— were all elusive. Like an alcoholic tired of trusting in the seemingly magical power of the bottle, I had reached the end of myself. I knew the only way to recover my soul was to admit that I was completely powerless. Only then could I find the healing power of God.

In some ways, my life changed dramatically after that ride home. I picked up my rarely used Bible and began to read and study the Scriptures. For a long time, I was overwhelmed with the words of God. It seemed like each time I read a verse, I heard the voice of God speaking directly to me. I still have that Bible and every once in a while, I look through it. The margins are full of notes and insights that God gave me.

As much as I'd like to say that everything got better overnight, I can't. My ulcers didn't miraculously disappear. For months, I endured slow and painful healing. The guilt over my girlfriend's abortion didn't vanish into thin air. Years later, I was still uncovering the deep wounds caused by that experience. I still struggled with lust, materialism, and feelings of inadequacy. I still didn't know what God wanted me to do with my life.

In fact, in many ways my pain *increased*. Part of this was because I had truly repented: I realized just how destructive and hurtful my sins were to myself and others. I knew of the widespread consequences of sin, that the repercussions can continue even after you're restored to God. But probably the biggest part of my pain was due to my desire to keep secrets. I believed that the restoration of my soul was a project that God and I could handle alone, without help from anyone else.

I did not seek the understanding and accountability of others in the body of Christ. To admit that I had problems would have meant revealing my sin to others. I only wanted to reveal God's holiness and character as He worked in my life— and not the sinfulness and depravity He was rooting out of my heart. I did not understand then that part of the transformation process involves vulnerability and accountability with a community of fellow believers. We are to tell and show each other the truth of our lives—both the holiness *and* the sin—so that we can shine God's light, His Word, into the world.

I chose to keep my struggles and inner conflicts to myself, even as I tried to get back on God's narrow path and serve Him with my life. After graduating from college, I decided to go to seminary. About the same time, I met a young woman and soon fell in love with her. But I did not understand the deeper issues in my life, and I failed to see what was really happening in the relationship. It was a one-sided relationship. As it turned out, she was not really in love with me, but perhaps she saw marriage as a better alternative than being alone. We married in 1975, but the relationship quickly unraveled. Just a few months into seminary and less than a year into our marriage, she left. I told my professors, even though I knew the school's policy: Anyone going through a divorce had to sit out a year. So that's what I did. That was an incredibly painful period in my life. I was confused because I had decided to serve God, which was why I had initially enrolled in seminary. Why would God block my path to serve Him? After all, I had been trying to live for Him for three years at that point.

Like my grandfather before me, I wrestled with suicidal thoughts. I simply did not know which way to turn. Even then, though, God had His hand on my life. As I mentioned before, I took a job as an aide in a psychiatric hospital for highly disturbed people, which soon led to my career in counseling. I learned the importance of honestly sharing and revealing thoughts, feelings, and tightly held secrets, so they can be brought into the light, wrestled over, and finally resolved. Secrets are, I believe, emotional and spiritual waste.

The Value of Openness

From a biblical perspective, keeping secrets is wrong. Secrets are almost always rooted in sin. When we keep secrets in our heart, then past sins and unresolved issues are allowed to fester, eating away at the soul and destroying our God-given potential. In many places, the Bible tells us to share our burdens with one another and speak the truth to each other. And there are a number of beneficial reasons we should do so. For example, in Ephesians, the apostle Paul writes about the purpose of the body of Christ and says that each of us should

> prepare God's people for works of service, so that the body of Christ may be built up until we all reach unity in the faith and in the knowledge of the Son of God and become mature, attaining to the whole measure of the fullness of Christ. Then we will no longer be infants, tossed back and forth by the waves, and blown here and there by every wind of teaching and by the cunning and craftiness of men in their deceitful scheming. Instead, speaking the truth in love, we will in all things grow up into him who is the Head, that is, Christ. (Ephesians 4:12–15)

Paul says here that the purpose of speaking the truth is so each one of us can reach full maturity in Christ, so that we can be fully prepared to serve God. In my own life, I was harboring dark secrets of paralyzing sin. The sin was connected to underlying and unresolved issues that drove me to look to places and things other than God for temporary relief. Because I didn't want to hear the truth, I remained immature in my faith and restricted in my ability to serve. My secrets were eating away at my soul.

Most of us would like to pretend that deep secrets in our lives don't exist. We would rather do anything than face the inevitable pain that comes from looking closely at our own souls. I think of a woman named Beth, because there are thousands of "Beths" running from their pain. Beth was one of the most active members in her church. She was involved in two or three ministries at a time and seemed to be there every time the church opened its doors. Yet Beth rarely followed through on the projects for which she volunteered. Usually, she would quit ministries in despair, frustrated and angry with the people to whom she ministered. Beth was trying to compensate for her own deeply rooted problems by "solving" the needs of others.

She had been raised in a home where her father sexually abused her as a teenager, sometimes several times a week. Beth tried to resolve her deep emotional needs by focusing on other people's needs—certainly a worthy and honorable goal. But she had not honestly faced her past, and caring for people was like pouring salt into her own wounds. She grew resentful that she was always sacrificing for others while her own wounds went untended.

Most people's problems are not as severe or traumatic as Beth's. But we all have obstacles to overcome. If we leave these wounds untreated, or pretend that they do not exist, they will only get worse.

As Christians, we have a profound responsibility to be honest with one another. We must both speak and listen—speak about problems and hurts inside of us, and listen to the problems and hurts of others. It is only then that true healing can begin.

Turning Pain into Purpose

Up until this point in this book, I have described how my life became bankrupt because I listened to the lies of the world. But, remarkably, God turned my pain into purpose, and my soul is now truly learning how to live, to feed on the love of God. And that is the focus of the next several chapters— how the God of second chances restores our shattered lives and souls.

My journey of restoration would have been stalled if I had not learned to be honest and open with Him and with fellow Christians. I'm not saying that we should share our most deep and intimate secrets at a church potluck. There are, of course, appropriate and inappropriate times to reveal ourselves to others. Vulnerability without the walls of trust is simply a form of exhibitionism. Still, all Christians need someone in their lives with whom they can share what is really going on inside. Whether it is your spouse, a trusted friend, a small group, a pastor, or a Christian counselor, there *must* be at least one person who knows the truth about you. The process of healing begins when we *admit* there is something that needs to be healed.

I'm not going to lie to you. If you've gotten off course and followed the wide road, then getting back to the narrow path will be painful. It was for me. As I look back on the process of how God turned my life around, I realize that with almost every good gift also came a painful challenge. My career is a good example. At the age of 32, I was chairman of a quarter-billion-dollar company. A year later, I had a trustee appointed for the near-bankrupt company, and I went in search of another job. The previous chairman had made some mistakes. There was no money for operations, and I had no way to fix things.

As I sought God's will, though, another "miracle" happened. A person who had followed my career with some interest approached me after hearing that the company I was working for went bankrupt. He asked, "If you had the money to start any company you wanted, what would you do?" I told him my dream of starting Christian counseling centers, so that people could begin to tap into the healing power of God. This man's partner was a Christian and both became excited about the idea. Within a few months, he had raised more than

$2 million. In November 1988, we started the New Life Treatment Centers. But as exciting as that prospect was, it occurred during a time when counseling agencies and psychiatric companies were bottoming out financially. It was almost as if God were saying, "I'm going to give you the dream of your heart, but you'll have to trust Me with it." I believe that He knows my tendency to fashion even good things into idols.

My marriage, too, has been a great blessing and a great challenge. I fell in love with Sandy almost immediately. I remember going into a restaurant after church one evening, sitting down at a table, and scanning the menu. Soon, I looked up to see an attractive couple seated at the table next to me, even though the restaurant was nearly deserted. So here was this cute girl and someone I presumed to be her boyfriend sitting next to me. Before long, she recognized me from our church, where I had been singing solos for about a year. I was embarrassed because I was alone and they looked as if they wanted to be alone, so I asked for the check as fast as I could and left. I later learned that when I walked out, the guy commented that it was interesting to be seated so close in the almost-empty restaurant. He wondered what God had in mind!

As it turned out, this fellow and Sandy had recently broken up and were just friends. The next

Sunday, I saw Sandy in church, and I was impressed with how attractive and full of life she was. I asked her out on Mother's Day. Not wanting any gaps in the conversation during our first date, I planned some small talk: I would tell her about my upcoming missions trip to India. Little did I know, Sandy was going on the same trip! We went out on a few more dates together, then on that outreach project halfway around the world. Quickly, it became apparent to me that Sandy was a person I couldn't live without—bright, talented, and gracious. We were married a year and a half after our first date.

Yet as big a blessing as our marriage has been, it has also been challenging. Early in our marriage, Sandy and I struggled with intimacy. It was hard work to learn to be vulnerable and completely open with each other. And then, just as we developed intimacy, it became clear that we could not have children. For years, we endured the humiliating procedures and tests of fertility clinics, but to no avail. Sandy did get pregnant once, but it was an ovarian pregnancy and could not be carried to term. To add to the pain, some Christians told me that Sandy and I were childless because God was punishing me for my girlfriend's abortion years earlier. But God, far from wanting to punish me, had greater things in store for us. He allowed us to adopt a wonderful little girl, and now it is impossible to imagine having a child we could love more.

God does not have a giant roulette wheel in the sky that determines our destiny. He brings events and circumstances into our lives that cause growth and maturity. God will certainly give us what we need, but what He most wants to give us is Himself. He longs for each one of us to be in a loving relationship with Him.

As God restores the soul, He also purifies our desires. He wants us to stop taking detours into the world's glittering paths of possessions, power, and pleasure. Instead, He wants us to stay on course and continue to move toward Him.

The narrow path leads us to living water, pure and deeply satisfying for our thirsty souls. I know. Even though the refining process has been painful, I have found that knowing God is the only thing in the world that I truly desire. When my heart is right with God, all of my other joys come naturally through worshiping Him.

Faith that Will Not Let Us Down

When I was a boy, my family lived in a house with a creek behind it. Being young, I didn't realize that frozen creeks could be dangerous. One day I tried to cross on the ice, and I fell through and into the freezing water below. My little overcoat froze, and I thought my mom would have to use an ice pick to remove it from me. I had unwisely put faith in that thin ice, and I broke through it. I didn't understand that the flowing water underneath prevented the ice from thickening.

Later on that same day, my brothers took me to a frozen pond behind a field near our house. Since the water wasn't running, the ice was frozen thick and solid. Yet even when my brothers would run on the ice to demonstrate its sturdiness, they had a difficult time convincing me that it would support my weight. I had been fooled by solid-looking ice before. Finally, they dragged me out onto the ice. At first, I tested it nervously. Then, slowly and hesitantly, I began to trust the ice. We played all afternoon on the thick ice, and no one fell through. That fun afternoon is one of my fondest childhood memories.

My experiences with ice remind me of the philosophies and teachings in which we put our faith. We have to test them to make sure they're truly trustworthy. Many things that look good on the surface may, in fact, put us in peril. Perhaps you have skated on the thin ice of faith in the world and its enticing lies. And you fell through, with chilling consequences. Now you don't know if you can trust anything or anyone, let alone develop the faith that Hebrews 11:1 talks about: "Now faith is being sure of what we hope for and certain of what we do not see." As opposed to trusting in the things of the world, which you can at least experience with the senses, God asks you to trust in things that you can't even see.

It is understandable that we're reluctant to sign over our complete trust to that which we are not certain of. But there is hope. First, the trust we offer God does not have to be that great to begin with. Jesus said that with just a mustard seed of faith, we could see impossible and tremendous things happen in our lives. Second, all you have to do is take one little step onto the ice. Test it—God will not fail us. Soon, we will be running across the ice, taking some painful falls, but as we are racing to the other side, joy will eventually overtake us.

Perhaps you have been wounded by the world by believing in the glittering lies of sin. Perhaps you are tremendously discouraged, bitter, and resentful. Perhaps you are dealing with childhood memories of abuse or abandonment. Or maybe you feel lonely and isolated. Maybe you live, like I did, with the unwelcome company of your own guilt and shame.

Whatever our situation, healing and growth will begin when we put our faith in God and, step by step, learn to place our full trust in Him. He will undergird us and support us, but the journey isn't always easy. By returning to God's narrow path, things might even get worse before they get better. But I want to emphasize that *things will get better.* If you truly have come to an end of yourself, this may, in fact, be the only time when you can successfully return to the path that follows God. In a sense, you are graced by your helplessness, because He will surprise you with His grace, His love, and His plan for your life.

TRUE FAITH

SET FREE *to* FOLLOW
THE NARROW PATH

During my junior and senior years in high school, I had a girlfriend named Sally. She was my first true love and everything any high school boy could want. She was a beautiful girl who had long blonde hair, an inviting smile, and a heart of laughter. Sally lived in a beautiful white house and had the best swimming pool in town. One summer, as she and her family were preparing to leave on vacation, her father asked me if I would take care of the pool, which looked like something the Romans would have constructed inside a fine palace. Always wanting to impress, I quickly agreed, considering it an honor somewhere up there with receiving the Purple Heart.

He took me to the pool and gave me instructions. He showed me how to test the water's pH level and how to take a sample of water and test it with chemicals from a pool kit. In a tube, the sample would turn various shades of pink. The kit also included a tube with the standard; if my shade of pink matched this shade of pink, then it meant the pool was perfectly chlorinated. If it was too dark, the pool had too much chlorine; too pale, it had too little.

"No problem," I reassured him. "Just leave it to me."

During the first week, I was diligent in my duties. The pink was always perfect. I imagined myself both a scientist and a lifeguard as I lounged around the pool. The second week, however, I became a little lax about the whole affair. In fact, I didn't even check on the pool until the day before Sally and her family were to come home. No problem, I reasoned. I had anticipated my absence by simply adding a bit more chlorine before I left. Clearly, this family was lucky to have such a clever and resourceful person taking care of their pool.

I'll never forget walking up to the edge of the pool that day. The water looked like milk (no exaggeration)! The sparkling blue-green color was gone. I took out the testing kit and mixed the chemicals. The results showed my sample as far from the middle as possible. To say that I had dumped too much chlorine in the pool was to say that Chernobyl leaked a little radiation. Sally's father had shown me what to do if there was not enough chlorine, but I had no idea what to do with too much. I needed to act fast and clear out the milk—or else. The next stage, I imagined, would be cottage cheese. I didn't want the family to come home to a chunky-style pool.

I called a friend of mine whose father owned a pool chemical company. I begged and pleaded for help. Could he get his dad to come and take a look? Much to my relief, his father agreed to rush over and see if there was anything he might do; he probably understood the dire condition of both myself and the pool. When he arrived, he looked at the creamy pool, shook his head a few times, and went to his truck. Returning, he dumped a few bags of something in the water. He said it was potash. I wasn't sure what potash was—I guessed that marijuana smokers collected their ash and sold it to pool companies—but I was sure grateful that it existed. Within hours, the pool returned to its crystal green, sparkling clarity.

I was there when Sally and her family returned home. I stood by the water, a regular pool magician. Her father smiled and thanked me. My girlfriend gave me a hug. The crisis had passed. Life was good again.

I mention this incident not so much to depict my irresponsibility, but to share the lesson I learned over those weeks: If you deviate from the standard, the established guidelines, you will pay the consequences. Like I stated before, as I journeyed off the narrow path in my life, I have had to learn that lesson time and again. Changing the standard doesn't alter our problems or remedy anything. If the shades of our actions deviate from the color of truth, we must change our actions, not try to alter the truth.

The Bible, the Word of God, is truth. It sets the ultimate standard. As such, the standard of truth is both impossibly bad and impossibly good news. It says that we are stained with sin, which sits dark and dismal in our hearts and minds. It says, too, that there is nothing we can do to make things right. But the good news is that though we cannot change our situation, there is One who can: God. Through the death and resurrection of Jesus Christ, our sins have been forgiven, death has been overcome, and a new life is possible for us.

Jesus said the truth would set us free. So why then do so many of us feel so bound up, so tied to guilt, addiction, abuse, or lust? Do you ever wonder how other people find deep and vital faith? Do you ever wonder if there's a formula, some prescription of faith that will bring freedom?

When I first came to Christ, I longed for freedom—from the past, from worry, from the consequences of sin. Just the thought that I might have a chance of experiencing it gave me a glimmer of hope in the midst of an increasingly dim and damaged life. But soon I was leaving the path of truth for the broad road of bright illusion and tickling half-truths.

"The truth will set you free" has become a battle cry that dedicated Christians often use to attract others to the faith. But if the truth really sets people free, why are there so many Christians in bondage? If the truth sets people free, why do power-hungry preachers abuse their people with legalistic and binding views? If the truth sets people free, why are so many people in the church trapped in abusive relationships? If the truth sets people free, why do we see so many dedicated men and women of God fall victim to sexual temptation and destroy their ministries and marriages?

Follow Me

Following Jesus means following the truth. Jesus made it clear: "I am the way and the truth and the life" (John 14:6). The way, the truth, and the life, then, are all connected in the person of Christ. You cannot follow Christ without following the truth, and you cannot have life—abundant life on earth and eternal life in heaven—without a relationship with Christ.

This is where the narrow path gets difficult. The truth, contrary to the voice of the world, is not relative and inclusive, bendable to fit our own desires. The truth is permanent and inflexible, both the demanding rigidity of the law and the relentless love of grace. John F. Kennedy said, "The greatest enemy of the truth is not the lie—deliberate, contrived, and dishonest, but the myth—persistent, pervasive, unrealistic." In our culture, two great and opposing myths prevail. One is the worship of self, which centers on the idea that there is a god inside each of us. The other extreme is the myth of fate, in which science tells us that we are controlled by our genes and our choices are determined by our inherited DNA codes. Both of these half-truths are twisted forms of the truth.

Although it is true that we were created to be "sons of God" (Romans 8:14), we do not become so through our own effort. And while it is true we are powerless to save ourselves, we are also free to obey and to live in the environment of grace (Romans 6:17). In the myths described above, the truth is twisted by impure motivation, founded on the need for power and control. One is blatant—I can do *anything*, and all I have to do is try. The other is subtle—I can do *nothing*, so I won't even bother. In both cases, the ultimate standard is the self. Such a demand for control, the Bible says, leads away from the truth. John 3:19 tells us, "This is the verdict: Light has come into the world, but men loved darkness instead of light because their deeds were evil." We would rather do anything (or nothing), it seems, than face up to the fullness of the facts.

The church is not immune to the influence of such powerful myths. Grace often seems anything but graceful. In His grace, God often reveals the destructive power of our own sin. This is a painful process. Because we often see pain as something that should be avoided at all costs, we begin to believe that God doesn't really know what He is doing. We would rather look and feel better than *be* better. We don't understand the good news that God loves us and wants us to be conformed to the likeness of His Son. So we demand control, often settling for less than the truth.

Obedience involves *choosing* to give up control. Deciding to love God and others and overcome self-obsession is what makes the narrow path so narrow. Having faith in Christ alone is hard work. The glittering and easy lies of the world seem so much more appealing than God's hard (but wonderful) promises. Jesus didn't make an empty promise when He spoke about the power of truth, but He did place a few conditions on its setting us free: "If you hold to my teaching, you are really my disciples. Then you will know the truth, and the truth will set you free" (John 8:31–32).

God's truth will free us; the problem is that we seek our own comfort and control instead of seeking love. Although it may not be an overt act of rebellion against God, we may find ourselves gradually drifting away from the truth that could free us. Living according to Christ's teachings makes us unashamed disciples who daily discover a deeper and richer knowledge of the truth. It is that knowledge that so counters the wisdom of the world and allows us to walk freely in God's love and grace. It enables us to find fulfillment, meaning, and purpose. The price of freedom is to trade in all the false teachings of the world and our self-constructed facades for a life of authentic Christianity.

We are to follow truth. And what path is that? Hebrews 12:2 points the way: "Let us fix our eyes on Jesus, the author and perfecter of our faith, who for the joy set before him endured the cross, scorning its shame, and sat down at the right hand of the throne of God."

Why are we so quick to believe what is false? Because we want to. We want to own, to possess, to hoard. And if we don't want actual power, we at least seek the power of certainty. Enough of this living-by-faith stuff. When we reach such a point, though, we have lost faith in God's love. We can find that love again through the truths of the Bible. But it is up to us to make choices based on the truth and then follow through. As 2 Timothy 3:16–17 states, "All Scripture is God-breathed and is useful for teaching, rebuking, correcting and training in righteousness, so that the man of God may be thoroughly equipped for every good work."

Truth and love are inseparable twins. Both seek to give, to free, to offer hope. They never seek to set their own broad path. Rather, truth and love follow Jesus on the narrow and self-giving road.

Grace to Be Honest

How can we remain faithful to truth if we are so predisposed to follow after soothing lies? First, we must believe the truth. We naturally tend to stray away from believing both the bad and good news of the gospel. We forget about God's grace and become impressed with ourselves. We lose touch with the deadliness of sin. We forget to be honest.

James 5:16 is a verse often ignored in contemporary churches: "Confess your sins to each other and pray for each other so that you may be healed." When was the last time you heard someone confess his or her sins in a church setting? It doesn't happen very often because people are too afraid they will become the next topic of the gossip chain. People don't reveal their problems, so others don't know how to pray for them. As a result, they remain in their broken condition, attending church, but not really being part of the church. When the gospel's bad news—that we are all sinners—is no longer a dynamic reality, we miss out on the gospel's good news—that we are all forgiven.

One couple I know stood up in front of their entire church and confessed their struggle with a particular sin. They admitted their fault and humbly begged forgiveness. Then they sat down. The other members of the church were stunned. No one had ever stood and confessed anything. After a few moments, some people clapped their hands, and soon the whole congregation was applauding. Their confession marked the beginning of a new church, a free church where healing was possible.

Just because we receive grace does not mean that we will never struggle with sin. Just the opposite. God gives us grace so we can more fully know and confess our sins to one another. The Bible is brutally honest about its "saints." There were no angelic editors assigned to take out the "bad" parts, to tidy up the records of the biblical figures. If we think the royals in England have had problems with their marriages over the past decade, it's nothing compared to the problems that David and his royal family had in the Bible. Adultery, murder, incest, and rape are all part of the biblical account of God's family. They are nothing new.

Despite the fact that problems are openly revealed throughout Scripture, the church has somehow gotten the notion that hiding is more important than healing. We put on happy faces and act like everything is wonderful. We fake it, then get into the car and go back home. We complain that we aren't getting what we need from church and criticize the staff for not doing a better job. Rather than change, we continue to live behind masks and play out our roles, trapped inside the illusions we have created to keep people from knowing who we really are.

We must understand and believe that through

repentance, grace removes sin, leaving us free and transformed. The myths of the world—that we are basically good or completely fated—disappear in the truth of God's grace.

A few years ago, I met with a suicidal woman at the request of her pastor. When she arrived at my office, she was one of the most distressed-looking people I had ever seen. I had been told she was a model at one time, but I couldn't see any evidence of it. My assistant took care of her three-year-old child while I attempted to provide some hope. The woman was full of venom and bitterness. I had never heard anyone more capable of spewing foul words. In between her expletives, I tried to get her to consider the issue of forgiveness—that she needed to both forgive others and allow God to forgive her.

This woman was convinced God had turned His back on her. Nothing I said made any difference. She responded to me as if I were a piece of wood. My attempts to communicate hope or a way out of her mess were futile. As she got up to leave, I made one last-ditch effort to help her. I reached over and took the wrapping off a new Life Recovery Bible and handed it to her. I told her that God's Word is far more powerful than anything I could say, and I encouraged her to take the Bible and read it. At that point, I could not imagine the slightest possibility that she would follow through. As I watched her walk out the door, I was convinced that I would get a call within the week, telling me she had taken her life.

Two months later, I was invited to preach at the church she attended. Just before the service, I saw a very attractive lady clutching a ragged-looking Life Recovery Bible. The suicidal woman had undergone an obvious and dramatic transformation. She had a smile on her face and a glint in her eyes.

When she approached me, I asked what she had done with herself. She looked at me and said, "I stopped believing the lies of Satan and started believing the truth of Jesus Christ."

She went on to say that she had spent a lot of time reading God's Word and going to church to learn more about the truth. It was one of the most joyous and fulfilling events of my life, a great surprise by God. By believing and living according to the truth, this woman was able to find hope in the midst of overwhelming problems.

If you are experiencing misery, despair, and hopelessness, perhaps it is because you have become confused about the truth. Perhaps it is because you have bought into some of the myths of this world. If you are willing to live by the truth, it will transform your life by giving you hope and confidence. Permanent, rock-solid, and never-changing, truth has the power to turn lives around.

The Soldier of Truth

What if we really believed the promises of God were true? What if we lived in faith that He would provide rest, shelter, food, love, forgiveness, and abundant life? Would we not be ready to bet our very lives on His words? Would we not be willing to take risks to love others and God more fully, with less anxiety and fear?

Of course we would. But in a fallen world, truth is never easy to follow, no matter how much faith we have. And as we've discussed, truth is not always something we care to hear. Jesus told His disciples that He would be betrayed by one of them, and sure enough, Judas proved that Christ was a man of His word. Peter also proved the truth of Christ's words when he denied his Lord. Jesus tells us similar truths about our own lives that we would rather not hear. He also tells us that, in a world bent on self-destruction, the truth will be despised. As fallen creatures, we forget that there is a source of absolute truth, and if we hold on to Him, we will find fulfillment and freedom.

All of us need to examine our lives and uncover the half-truths, myths, and encumbrances that stand in the way of our relationship with God. Is it money? Is it lust? Is it alcohol? Is it power? It's important to be aware of the sin that hinders us from achieving Christ's call on our lives. To me, one of the most frightening scriptures speaks of people who believe they are serving God but really aren't. Christ tells us that when He returns, some people who claim to have been serving Him will say, "I have done great things in Your name, Lord. I have healed people. I have prophesied." Christ will say to them, "I never knew you" (see Matthew 7:21–23). They thought they had it. But in the hot light of God's truth, their false idols melt.

A couple of years ago, the movie *Clear and Present Danger* appeared in theaters. I remember that a bus went through our town displaying an ad for this movie that read, "Truth Needs a Soldier." When I saw that, I reflected that our world would be so different if more Christians would decide to be soldiers of the truth—to live for the truth, fight for the truth, and even die for the truth. If Christians became more dedicated soldiers, they could change the world from a painful and empty place to one of fulfillment and freedom.

The challenge is to live according to the truth, no matter what. To be a person of truth requires a commitment to act beyond our feelings and desires for immediate gratification and put the foundations of our faith into action. *True* faith results in love. We become loving people not by *believing* more in love but by *showing* more love, even when we don't feel like it. We become servants not by believing in the concept of servanthood but by seeking to honor God by meeting the needs of others, even if it is unpleasant. When we dedicate ourselves to living according to God's truth, we will not only transform our own lives but the world as well.

CHAPTER TEN

DENY THE WORLD

*L*EARNING *to* HOLD
THINGS LOOSELY

I looked up at the hills surrounding my town and watched, along with my coworkers, the firestorm rip through the beautiful hills of Laguna Beach. The fires had already destroyed more than 200 homes on the north side of the town. We watched in total silence—both awed and fearful at the sight.

I left the office early that day—on an otherwise beautiful morning in October 1993. Our home, the one Sandy and I had lovingly established 10 years earlier, was in the path of the fire. On my drive home, I confessed to the Lord about my struggle with materialism. I prayed some dangerous prayers: *Lord, help me to release my grip on things*. Later that day, as Sandy and I began to load belongings into our two cars and our friend Burt Wilson's Toyota pickup, we could see the fire slowly creep toward our street. With such little space and time, we faced critical decisions about what we considered valuable.

I was surprised at how little I really cared about. God had obviously been working in my life. The first thing I loaded into the trunk of my car was my collection of ukuleles. Having fought against depression a good deal of my life, I had learned a valuable lesson: It is almost impossible to be depressed while playing a ukulele. Next, I helped Sandy pack photos and videotapes—priceless and irreplaceable snapshots of our lives together.

I couldn't think of anything else I wanted to save. Ukuleles, snapshots, videos, and the three of us—Sandy, two-and-a-half-year-old Madeline, and myself. What else really mattered?

I climbed onto the roof of my house and doused it with water, even though I knew it probably wouldn't do any good. I could see some of the other houses on our street already starting to burn. There were no fire trucks—not even the sound of a far-off siren—as they had all been dispatched to other locations. Only the hungry sound of fire broke the silence. There was clearly no hope of saving our home.

Sandy took Madeline in one of the cars, and we agreed to meet at the McDonald's in Dana Point, just a short distance away. As I desperately watered my roof, the police arrived, their bullhorns blaring.

"The fires are burning on this street!" the officers announced. "You must abandon your homes and leave, or you might not be able to."

The whole town was being evacuated. I could see a huge tanker aircraft flying overhead, dropping fire retardant. I climbed down from the roof and decided to make a final search of the house. Had we forgotten anything of value? I ran, looking through each room, but didn't find anything. While rushing for the front door, I saw out of the corner of my eye a small, shiny, green vinyl, froggy purse—Madeline's prized possession. It cost maybe $2.50. Acting on impulse, I tucked the purse under my arm and locked the front door. Climbing into my car, I tossed the purse into the back seat.

I drove away from our house, overwhelmed with grief. Even though my search hadn't revealed anything else worth taking, it was still painful to think of all our worldly possessions going up in smoke, not to mention our beloved house. We would be stripped of something dear to us. Sure, it was just wood, vinyl, and glass, but it had been our home for a decade.

When I arrived at McDonald's, I found my wife and little girl. Sandy was understandably upset since she believed, as I did, that everything in our house was about to be incinerated. Madeline was upset because Sandy was upset. We decided to spend the night with my mother-in-law. Because Sandy was so distraught, I decided Madeline would ride with me. I strapped her into the seat beside me.

While we were driving, she looked up at me and asked in her little-girl way, "Daddy, house burned down?"

"Madeline, we don't know if it burned down. We won't know for a couple of days."

All at once, a horrible, sad look appeared on Madeline's face.

"Daddy," she whispered. "Forgot my froggy purse."

With one eye on the road, I reached around into the back seat. My hand found that green, cheap piece of shiny vinyl. I handed it to her—and I became an instant hero.

A huge grin covered her face as she hugged my right arm and said, "Thank you, Daddy."

At that moment, I wouldn't have taken $20,000 for that ridiculous little purse.

Fortunately for us, Madeline's purse wasn't the only thing that survived our near tragedy. Our entire house was spared. Just after I had left our house, the fire department decided that if they didn't stop the fire at our street, the houses down the hill would burn because most of them had wooden roofs. And if that happened, the fire would have continued to burn out of control, putting the whole town in jeopardy. The firemen made a daring and courageous stand. Just 10 houses away from ours, they stopped the progress of the fire.

In the shadow of that awful blaze, God taught me an invaluable lesson: the kingdom principle of what's really valuable. So close to having all of my belongings consumed by a raging inferno, I discovered that there are very few things I can't live without. Of course it would have been difficult, perhaps even devastating, to lose our house and its contents. But through that I learned they're just things, and they matter very little in the grand scheme of life. I had discovered how to hold things loosely. Doing that, I discovered freedom.

Discarding Idols

Things, in and of themselves, possess no special power. Like the deaf, dumb, and mute idols spoken of in Psalms, their power is not in an internal magic, but in their ability to captivate people's hearts and minds. The Bible frequently records God speaking against the power of idols, as He did through the prophet Hosea: "They consult a wooden idol and are answered by a stick of wood" (4:12).

Sometimes our things, our idols, help us to worship ourselves. As Habakkuk 2:18 says, "Of what value is an idol, since a man has carved it? Or an image that teaches lies? For he who makes it trusts in his own creation; he makes idols that cannot speak." When we fashion idols, we are trusting in our own creation rather than in God.

The Ralph Lauren Polo shirts and the gold Rolex watch that I wore were only as powerful as my desire for them. As God began to convict me of the hold materialism had on me, I foolishly believed that if I simply got rid of the things—or at

least replaced them with items of lesser value—
that my problem would be eliminated. So I
exchanged my Rolex for a runner's watch, my big
Mercedes-Benz for a beat-up Volkswagen, and my
Ralph Lauren shirts for some from The Gap.

The Volkswagen, which I drove for years, was
especially "unmaterialistic." It was an ugly color—
something like a gray sky in the midst of a smog
alert—and had no power steering, no power brakes,
and very little power under the hood. It gave me terrible neck aches. Driving it made me feel as if I were
doing some kind of penance. What I had done, in my
battle against materialism, was to exchange one
image for another. But that never really cured me. I
never stopped to examine the underlying issues of
envy, greed, disappointment, and anger that were
driving my lust for things. Even if we live in virtual
poverty, materialism can still have a deep hold on us.

A few months before the fire that nearly
destroyed our home, I remember having a conversation with a trusted and loving friend, Jim Burns.
I was about to admit, for the first time, that I struggled with materialism.

"Jim," I began, "do you ever wonder why I've dri-
ven that beat-up Volkswagen around all these years?"

"Come to think of it, I have wondered about
that," Jim replied. "Why do you?"

"I drive it because I'm one of the most materialistic people that you'll ever meet in your life."

Jim thought for a moment. "Well, driving that Volkswagen, you sure don't *look* very materialistic," he said.

I took a deep breath. "Jim, that's exactly why I've been driving that car. It's part of a big facade. Seeing me in that Volkswagen, you'd never dream that I was materialistic in my heart."

We talked more about how I had gotten off the narrow path and onto the wide road where things mean more than they should. It was not something I had wanted anyone to know, but once the big secret was out, I immediately began to experience some changes in that area of my life. Facing the lie and admitting my struggle to someone else was the first step back to living according to the truth.

When God confronts us with sin in our lives, we can always be tempted to make superficial changes—to cover up the symptom instead of dealing with the root problem. But, as I've discussed, the greatest enemy to real and lasting change is to keep secrets. I kept the secret of my materialism hidden behind a beat-up Volkswagen, but I was just as consumed with accumulating things as a man with a garage full of fancy cars.

Greed Can Sabotage Relationships

The disease of materialism can become especially virulent if left hidden and untreated. The Bible says that it is impossible to "love money and God."

The disease is fatal to genuine spirituality. In my own life, I have learned that the real power of materialism is in its ability to divert our hearts from what really matters, such as building loving relationships. When we love money and the things it can buy, we begin to focus our hearts on acquiring. In such a diseased heart, other people become a means to an end. We will hold them in esteem only if they can increase our net value. It is not surprising, then, that instead of connecting me to the right people, materialism disconnected me from nearly everyone.

A materialistic lifestyle is, if nothing else, a lonely existence. More times than not, a materialistic person uses others rather than loves them. I recently read an article that chronicled the lives of the richest and most powerful men in the early part of the twentieth century. In 1923, at the Edgewater Beach Hotel in Chicago, nine of these men met with one goal in mind: to corner the financial markets of the world. At that time, the men gathered around the conference table had more accumulated wealth than the federal government. They had, almost literally, the world at their fingertips.

During the years that followed that meeting, all of these men were relegated to the sad and bizarre footnotes of history. Here is the fate of these nine men, once the most powerful in the country:

- Charles Schwab, a steel magnate, died bankrupt, having lived his last five years on borrowed money;

- Samuel Insel, president of the largest utility company in America, died penniless and a fugitive from justice;

- Howard Hopkins, president of the largest American gas company, went insane;

- Arthur Cotton, a great food speculator, died insolvent overseas;

- Richard Whitney, president of the New York Stock Exchange, served time in Sing Sing prison;

- Albert Fall, a cabinet member for the U.S. government, was pardoned from prison so he could die at home;

- Ibar Krueger, who headed up the world's largest land monopoly, committed suicide;

- Leon Fraiser, president of the International Settlement, committed suicide;

- Jesse Livermore, stock speculator, committed suicide.

What strikes me about this list is not so much that most of these men died poor, but that they died alone. Their money and power—the idols of their own creation—were truly impotent, deaf, and blind to their real needs. In their dying whispers, I can hear the message of another rich man, a king by the name of Solomon: "Meaningless! Meaningless! . . . Everything is meaningless. What does man gain from all his labor at which he toils under the sun?" (Ecclesiastes 1:2–3).

We have all heard how some rich people treat others like things. Heddy Green, for example, died the world's richest woman in the 1950s by accumulating more than $100 million. She was infamous for her ruthless, penny-pinching life. When her son had a bad knee, Heddy dressed herself and her son in rags so that she could receive free treatment at the local hospital. When a doctor recognized her and told her that she would have to pay up, she refused. Her son's leg eventually had to be amputated because his rich mother was too stingy to pay for treatment.

Someone recently told me about a man named Mark, whose closest relationships were ruined by his greed. At the age of 22, he left his wife when she gave birth to their son. When the child was six months old, Mark came back and held the boy in his arms. He decided to leave again. "For the amount of money this kid would cost me," he told an acquaintance, "I could have a Lamborghini."

We might be tempted to say, like the self-righteous Pharisee, "Thank God I am not one of *them*."

But what we don't realize, or refuse to realize, is how deeply the culture of materialism has affected us all. Living in a culture that is fueled by greed and competition, we are all vulnerable to worshiping at the altar of money and things, often in subtle ways. How many of us treat the company vice president differently than we treat the janitor? How many of us, when we choose our friends, are not influenced by a title or a ski boat or the size of a home? How many of us, when we see something that another person has, secretly believe that we deserve to have it, too?

When Jesus tells us to deny the world, He is not talking about selling everything we have, moving to a commune, and eating only pork and beans. Nor is He telling us that things are necessarily bad. What He is saying is not to let those things burrow into our hearts and feed our envy and greed. When we allow things to become our focus, we lose sight of our real purpose—to love God and to love others.

Jesus wants us to be light on our feet, stripped of the things we think we need, which in reality only weigh us down. We must seek to be like Jesus. In Matthew 8:20, He says, "Foxes have holes and birds of the air have nests, but the Son of Man has no place to lay his head." Jesus did not allow things to constrain Him from wholeheartedly serving His heavenly Father. He let nothing distract Him from His mission on earth. Although I don't believe we need to sell our houses and carry only a sleeping bag, the principle is certainly one we should follow. That is, we should examine our lives to see if there's anything that keeps us from total, unrestrained service to the Lord.

The writer of Hebrews says that we should seek to travel lightly on our spiritual journey: "Let us throw off everything that hinders and the sin that so easily entangles, and let us run with perseverance the race marked out for us" (12:1). God *does* want us to have fulfillment and purpose, which is why He asks us to hold our possessions loosely. The abundant life He offers comes from living for those things that bring lasting joy.

Two hundred years ago, archeologists decided to dig up the remains of Charlemagne, known as Charles the First, the Frankish king who lived from 742 to 814. In his tomb, Charlemagne sat on a golden throne in a golden sepulcher, surrounded by gold and jewels. He was clothed in cloth made from gold and silver thread. One of the workmen excavating the tomb looked at the long-dead king sitting in all his grandeur and said, "Man, that is living."

On the king's knee a Bible was placed, a bony finger pointed to Mark 8:36: "What good is it for a man to gain the whole world, yet forfeit his soul?"

CHAPTER ELEVEN

Deny Yourself

Giving Ourselves Away for The Sake of Others

A few years back, I went on a business trip to Fairbanks, Alaska. I went in January—not the best time to visit Alaska. During the winter in Fairbanks, the sun never comes up, and the cold is deeper and more penetrating than you can imagine. After landing at the airport, which was covered with a light-blue permafrost, I walked off the airplane and into 40-below temperature. I could barely breathe. Before I could take my rental car, the attendant had to unplug the engine heater (used to keep the fluids from freezing).

Checking into my hotel, I made my way to the restaurant to grab a bite to eat. While I was eating, a man came in and sat down at the table next to me. His cologne arrived a couple of seconds before he did. But that's not all he exuded. He had the air of a rich man about him. For some reason, I remember exactly how this man looked, right down to the finest detail: a navy blazer with bright gold buttons; the kind of Italian loafers that wealthy people wear, which make their feet look a couple of sizes smaller; a flashy gold watch; perfectly coifed hair; and a steady, firm gaze.

As I eyed this man, he would occasionally glance my way, and I would act as if I hadn't seen him. In my mind, I was judging him, dismissing him as an arrogant, pompous man. *Oh, brother,* I snickered to myself. *Look at this guy. He really thinks he's something.*

Slyly watching the man, I noticed him call the wine steward to his table. Not surprisingly, he ordered a bottle of the best red wine in the house. The wine steward was obviously excited, working hard to display whatever charm he possessed. I imagined he was thinking, *Big tip!* After the steward uncorked the bottle, the man took it and inhaled the aroma. I wondered how he could smell anything over his powerful cologne. Next, the steward poured some wine into what looked like a baby rattle that hung from his neck. He was tasting the wine for the man, as if he were the cupbearer for King Nebuchadnezzar and there was risk that some conspirator might poison him. The steward then poured a little into a glass for the man, who swirled it around and sniffed the wine. Then he threw his head back and rolled it around in his mouth. He looked like he was about to gargle. I thought, *If he doesn't like it, he's going to spit it out all over me and everyone around him.* I scooted over a bit just in case.

It was fascinating. This man was totally immersed in the ritual. It must have been good wine, for with a nod of his head to the steward, his glass was filled. Next, he made a motion with his arm, and the steward leaned over as the rich man whispered something in his ear. Unexpectedly, the steward picked up the wine bottle, put it on his tray, and set out across the dining room.

I looked around and saw several attractive women on the other side of the room. *Great,* I thought. *In addition to this guy smelling like the cologne counter at Saks Fifth Avenue, now he's acting like a shark smelling a kill.* He could probably harpoon any woman's heart with his money and charm. I was starting to lose my appetite.

Beyond the good-looking women, I noticed an elderly woman sitting by herself in the corner. She was overweight, and her face was leathery. She had matted hair and wore a tattered old coat with an ugly scarf. I wondered how she could let herself be seen like that in a public place.

As I returned my gaze to the steward, I watched him walk past one beautiful woman, and then another. My eyes stayed one step ahead of him, trying to guess which attractive woman would be the "lucky" one tonight. Which of these ladies would be the recipient of this man's gift? Much to my surprise, the steward stopped at the table of the elderly, disheveled woman. He whispered something in her ear, which seemed to embarrass her. Then he poured her a glass of wine. With that, he stepped back. The old woman held up her glass and looked over at the rich man, who raised his glass in return. Across the room, they shared a toast from the best bottle of wine in the house.

I have thought about that moment often—not only about my own critical, judgmental attitude toward both the rich man and the old woman, but also how the scene was a metaphor of grace. Who could imagine such a gift on that cold, dark night in the deep Alaska winter? This rich man could have chosen any number of beautiful women to charm and entice, but instead he lavished an expensive gift on a wrinkled old lady dressed in rags. What would possess him to do such a thing? What a surprising, unselfish act!

The man's generosity reminded me of God's grace toward each of us. He owns the cattle on a thousand hills. He created the cosmos, arranged the millions of stars that sparkle in the sky, and has the power to control every atom and molecule. And yet He gives us every good and perfect gift. He could have chosen only the beautiful people, the put-together people to receive His blessings. But instead, He says, "I have chosen the lowly, the foolish, the weak, and the despised people of the world" (see 1 Corinthians 1:27–29). While we were still sinners, Christ died for us, shedding His blood, the wine of the New Covenant.

But that was only the beginning of God's gifts to us. Here is just a partial list of His surprises:

□ *"New birth into a living hope through the resurrection of Jesus Christ from the dead"* (1 Peter 1:3);

□ *"His glorious grace, which he has freely given us in the One he loves"* (Ephesians 1:6);

□ Salvation and the call to a holy life— *"not because of anything we have done but because of his own purpose and grace"* (2 Timothy 1:9);

□ *"Different gifts, according to the grace given us"* (Romans 12:6);

□ *"Everything we need for life and godliness through our knowledge of him who called us by his own glory and goodness"* (2 Peter 1:3);

□ All of His *"great and precious promises, so that through them [we] may participate in the divine nature and escape the corruption in the world caused by evil desires"* (2 Peter 1:4);

□ *"The Spirit as a deposit, guaranteeing what is to come"* —righteousness, eternal life, heaven, and adoption as children of God (2 Corinthians 5:5).

Who Would Reject God's Gifts?

Suppose that in the restaurant where I witnessed the rich man's surprising generosity, the elderly, overweight woman, after sipping the best wine in the house, spit it out. Then she reached into her purse, pulled out a bottle of Mad Dog 20/20, and proceeded to get drunk. She then staggered over to that rich man, took a sniff of his cologne, and vomited on his shoes. She sneered at him and then went outside, where she passed out in the subzero temperature and froze to death in minutes.

It would be hard to even imagine such a thing—such a cold, muddle-headed, insane rejection of a wonderful gift given in a spirit of love and grace. I suspect, by now, that you know where I am headed. My point is that many Christians spurn the gifts that God has so freely given us. In fact, in one of my more honest moments, I finally came to see that I had spent most of my Christian life sneering at God and disregarding the things He offered. I had taken the great gifts that He had lavished on me and squandered them in futile pursuits of self-fulfillment.

I try not to be too hard on myself. We are all born sinners right down to the bone. Given a choice and left to our own devices, which God certainly allows, we will choose lust over love 99 times out of 100. As the Old Testament prophet Jeremiah laments, "The heart is deceitful above all things and beyond cure. Who can understand it?" (17:9).

We must come to recognize our uncanny ability to sin and the destruction that comes from it. We must clearly see how much we desire to seek after counterfeits, settle for mediocrity, and turn our backs on God's grace. Like a surveyor after a hurricane, we must honestly assess the cost of sin and destruction. It is never easy to view depravity from the inside, but we must in order to begin getting beyond it. I was lucky: God brought me to a place where I could not deny my own sin and the destruction that it had caused. Many people never get there. Crushed and able to see who I really was, I found myself in a position to truly repent, fully accept His grace, and move toward restoration.

Self-Denial Is Not a Popular Concept

When you speak of denying yourself in our society, you are looked upon as the equivalent of a Neanderthal with a gimp leg—what could be more backward, repressed, and antiquated? People laugh at your ignorance and tell you to lighten up and join the modern world. You will not find the principle of denying self in any humanistic, secular psychology book. It is not a popular theory on how to find fulfillment. In fact, just the opposite has occurred; the focus is more on denying *others* than on denying yourself. The modern creed has become, "I'll take as much as I can get!"

Selfishness makes the headlines every day. A man sues because his rights have been violated. A woman conducts another wildly successful "me-first" seminar. Another princess gets a divorce. A company, already making a healthy profit, restructures and lays off thousands of loyal workers. A local union goes on strike, demanding better pay and job security. A government official takes a golf vacation at the taxpayers' expense. If you want more examples of man's self-serving ways, pick up a newspaper or watch the television news. Our world is trembling in the grip of selfish, angry demands.

In their quest for self-fulfillment, people often go to absurd and even comical extremes. An example is the Psychic Friends Network, the number one revenue-generating TV infomercial. The format, as I understand it, works something like this: People call in to total strangers and expect to find deep answers about themselves and their future. Recently, a friend of mine was at dinner with an administrator of the Psychic Friends Network. The man took a break from dinner to find out how the infomercial was working that night. Out of 1,000 counselors on the network, all but two were on the phone, generating money at the rate of $3.50 a minute. Literally thousands and thousands of people were calling for answers.

We live in a disconnected, post-modern world,

where science and reason have increasingly failed to meet their lofty promises. As a result, we turn to all kinds of weird, feel-good theology, none of which is based on any truth or logic. We are getting in touch with our guardian angels—tender, white-blue creatures who love us and are as soft as teddy bears. We are reading horoscopes and channeling spirits to find out how to "get ahead." We are buying books and attending seminars to discover the secret of striking it rich. All this is done in an effort to find self-fulfillment, and all of it without a hint of self-sacrifice or such "old-fashioned" words as *discipline, repentance, truth,* or *responsibility.*

The self-actualization movement says, "Rely only on yourself; you don't need help from anyone else." The fundamental principle is that the more you actualize yourself, using more and more of your potential, the more fulfilled you will become. I believe self-actualization is the greatest oxymoron. Recently, I read the book *Man's Search for Meaning* by Viktor Frankl, who was a survivor of the Holocaust.[1] I read it after spending a day at the holocaust museum in Washington, D.C. He is a great writer and one of the most respected minds in the area of psychology. During that horrible period of his life, he observed how people lived and died. Frankl noted that those who let life slip away did so because they had nothing to live for. He powerfully describes the bankruptcy of "self-actualization." In his book, he writes, "The more one forgets himself by giving himself to a cause to serve or another person to love, the more human he is and the more he actualizes himself. What is called self-actualization is not an attainable aim at all for the simple reason that the more one would strive for it, the more one would miss it. In other words, self-actualization is possible only as a side effect of self-transcendence."

Jesus made a similar point when He said, "I tell you the truth, unless a kernel of wheat falls to the ground and dies, it remains only a single seed. But if it dies, it produces many seeds. The man who loves his life will lose it, while the man who hates his life in this world will keep it for eternal life" (John 12:24–25). Jesus demonstrated this in His own life when He died so we could live forever.

That's the paradox of true joy. The more you strive to actualize yourself, the more you lose the potential to find the meaning you desire. Only when you deny yourself and serve others in love will you experience true meaning and fullness.

Jesus' Example of Self-Denial

Jesus provides the best model of self-sacrifice and obedience. Hebrews 5:8 attests to this: "Although he was a son, he learned obedience from what he suffered." I have often pondered what that verse means. Didn't Jesus just naturally do what God wanted Him to do? His prayer in Gethsemane reveals that He did not. He prayed, "Not as I will, but as you will" (Matthew 26:39). Jesus did not *want* to die on the cross. He did not want divine wrath to descend on Him for every sin ever committed. But He obeyed. His obedience, though, was not a dismal, barren, cosmic slaughter. He endured the cross, the Bible tells us, "for the joy set before him" (Hebrews 12:2). Through His obedience, Christ gave the ultimate example of self-sacrifice: He died to give others life.

Because we are not God, or even gods (contrary to the teaching of some New Age gurus), we have even more reason to follow Jesus' example and deny ourselves. Unlike Jesus, we are not sinless. Our human hearts yearn for comfort, control, and self-seeking. In order to keep from squandering God's great and wonderful gifts on our cheap, small selves, we must learn to give ourselves away in love and service. By obeying, we rework our attitude to be like that of Jesus. "Do nothing out of selfish ambition or vain conceit, but in humility consider others better than yourselves. Each of you should look not only to your own interests, but also to the interests of others" (Philippians 2:3–4).

As Christians, we love to hear the scriptures about freedom, but we hate to hear the parts about obedience. God demands compliance from His followers, not because He wants us to be miserable, but because He wants us to *avoid* misery. Obeying

His laws protects us from the misery we experience when we stray outside His limits. Jesus said the entire Law comes down to two commands: Love God and love others (see Matthew 22:37–39). Through obedience, we learn to deny ourselves and love others. Obedience is never easy. We learn to acquire the attitude of a servant.

Recently, I spoke at a conference in Denver. I delivered my message, which contained some thoughts about serving one another, and I prepared to leave the conference and head for the airport. I was exhausted and anxious to be home.

I was about to get into my car when I recognized a man coming toward me. He was not someone I wanted to talk to, especially given how tired I was. A few years back, this man had worked for me in one of our psychiatric treatment centers before he was caught in an extramarital affair. He had caused me and the other employees a great deal of embarrassment and pain. As he approached, my initial urge was to hop in my car and drive away, but I felt God nudging me to stay and talk. I did an about-face and walked toward the man.

"I came to this conference just to talk with you," he said.

Hesitantly, I agreed to chat for a few minutes. He seemed relieved that I didn't turn my back and leave him standing there.

"Steve, I want you to know how sorry I am

about the way I messed up . . . for my sin. I'm in the process of restoration and rehabilitation, and part of that process is seeking your forgiveness." He looked me in the eye and said, "I apologize for the pain I caused you and others. I ask your forgiveness."

It was obvious that God was working in this man's life. Fortunately, rather than avoid him, I was obedient to God's leading, and I was able to offer this man forgiveness and love. As a result, I trust that God used me to help him heal. It was a wonderful moment for both of us.

What Self-Denial Requires

A servant must have an attitude of love. We can only love, the Bible tells us, because we were first loved by God. Unfortunately, when we obey God's call to give ourselves away, it is often because we feel that we *have* to, or because we want to portray the *image* of a good person, or because that is simply what a Christian is supposed to do. This is lifeless, joyless obedience. Unless our obedience springs from knowing God's deep love for us, we will simply be going through the motions of keeping rules.

It is our rebellion and self-obsession that break off our love relationship with God. When we keep Him at a safe distance, we sacrifice the very things we are seeking. Isaiah 48:17–18 says, "I am the Lord your God, who teaches you what is best for you, who directs you in the way you should go. If only you had paid attention to my commands, your peace would have been like a river, your righteousness like the waves of the sea."

We must reconnect ourselves to God's awesome love. Read about and experience His greatest love letter to us, Jesus Christ. And, like the apostle John, consider "how great is the love the Father has lavished on us, that we should be called children of God! And that is what we are!" (1 John 3:1).

When we discover and rediscover the love of God, we will be more likely to trust Him. And trust is the basis of obedience—a commitment to do what is right over what is comfortable, to step out of our obsessions and addictions, and to use whatever we have been given to serve others and to serve God. Turn the wonderful and great gifts God has given you into acts of service. And then sit back and savor the taste of the best wine in the house, the fruit of having a servant's heart.

CHAPTER TWELVE

GIVING AND SERVING

INVESTING *in* THINGS THAT REALLY MATTER

A few years back, Sandy and I were invited to a special wedding. The father of the bride, Hal Asher, was a dear and treasured friend. When the invitation arrived, both of us wanted to purchase the most expensive wedding gift we had ever bought, and that is exactly what we did—as much to show respect for Hal as to help the young couple.

Sandy and I had met Hal when his advertising agency handled the account for a company where I had worked. For some reason, he liked us and helped us survive the first difficult years of our marriage. When we were really struggling, Hal gave Sandy and me an all-expenses-paid vacation to the Caribbean. No one had ever done anything like that for us, and no one has done it since. Hal always went out of his way to encourage us.

Hal was a successful and busy man. He had dined with many stars who had worked with him on commercials, and he knew how to entertain people royally. When he heard that my parents were coming to town for a visit, he insisted on taking them out to dinner at a restaurant near his

Beverly Hills home. For my parents, who lived in rural Texas, a Beverly Hills dinner with the head of an advertising agency was a once-in-a-lifetime experience. After arriving at Hal's home, where we ate enough hors d'oeuvres to constitute an entire meal, we were off to The Palm restaurant for a dinner that my parents never forgot. Hal ordered for all of us since he had been there many times. When the food arrived, my folks could not believe their eyes. Set before them were two huge lobsters, weighing about 20 pounds each. One claw on those lobsters was bigger than any whole lobster I have ever eaten. My dad ate and ate and smiled and laughed and ate and told his corny jokes and ate more until he had devoured the entire lobster.

For the rest of my father's life, he continued to talk about that evening. As a storyteller, he probably got more mileage out of that one evening than any other single event in his life. Needless to say, I am forever indebted to Hal Asher for giving my father one of the greatest evenings of his life, not to mention all the other things he did for Sandy and me.

So when we learned that this dear man's daughter was getting married, Sandy and I wanted to honor him, and we could not do that by scrimping on our gift. We spent more money than we had, but the sacrifice was worth it. He recognized we had done something special—not so much for the bride, whom we hardly knew, but to show our appreciation to him.

From that wedding, I learned a valuable lesson that applies to my spiritual life: You can't throw pennies at the bride and expect the father to be honored. Mediocre, perfunctory, or hand-me-down gifts simply won't get the job done. For a gift to be of real value, given from the heart, only a gift that requires sacrifice will do.

Generous Gifts for the Bride

The New Testament frequently refers to the church as the Bride of Christ. As members of the church, we have been given precious and valuable gifts that God desires us to use sacrificially for the Bride of Christ. But don't we often give to the bride only what is convenient? We look for flashy, big, and expensive-looking things or we dig through our spiritual cedar chests for a token we can toss at the bride's feet. When we offer only casual and convenient gifts to the church, Christ's bride, how do you think that makes the Father feel?

The wedding of Hal Asher's daughter caused me to rethink my view of the church. The church is more than just another organization committed to good and moral causes. It's a living, divine organism, which calls us to give not only our gifts, but also to give our very selves.

When Jesus asked Peter if he loved Him, Peter replied three times that, of course, he did. And after each response, Jesus told Peter to "feed my sheep." Jesus meant that as proof of his love, Peter should care for and nurture His church, His precious and lovely bride. Jesus did not tell Peter to start something big or build some spectacular building. He didn't tell him to use his organizational skills to start a massive movement. His instructions for showing love were simple: Take care of my bride. The same standard applies to all of us. Are we giving our gifts—our money, time, or energy—to the church as an act of love for God?

We often judge churches by a great many standards—by the number of members, by the number of ministries, by the quality of outreach programs, by the pastor's reputation, and so on. But the one true standard of the church should be this: Are its people giving sacrificially and serving others out of love for God? Even though it is faith that saves us, it is service to others that fulfills us.

My father would not have been considered a wealthy man by many standards, but he was one of the richest men I know. His life was a model of service to the church and other people. One of the earliest memories I have of my father was when he took our family to the "wrong side of the tracks" to help needy people. We would carry food to those who lived in one-room houses, many of which had no source of heat. We didn't have much money ourselves, but we still gave to those who had less. My father taught me many valuable lessons in servanthood.

Near the end of his life, he was still serving. After my brother Jerry died of AIDS, my father (and my mother) visited prisons and hospitals where people were dying of AIDS. In those places, he would share God's love and the good news of the gospel. My father could have easily lost himself in the pain of his son's homosexuality; he could have turned away from those who had the same disease that took one of his boys. But my father was wiser and richer than that. He knew that life, real and true life, comes in service to others.

My dad died a few years ago, at age 68, from a massive heart attack. At his funeral, the pastor mentioned the balance between faith and works.

"When it came to the life of Walter Arterburn," he said, "there was never any question or doubt about whether faith or works were more important. In his life, he had incredible faith, and he put it to work serving people."

My father rarely lost sight of what was real. It wasn't the stuff of the world—what you could touch, feel, hear, smell, and see—that was important and real, but what was invisible, the unseen qualities of love, faith, grace, and hope. He knew that giving of himself—his kindness and service as well as his money—was what really mattered. By giving, he received much in return.

When It's Difficult to Serve

The narrow path that Jesus prescribed for us is traveled very slowly, on our knees in service to others. Many people in the church, however, find this difficult to do. Sometimes people erroneously believe that serving others is an "answer" to their own hardships. They serve dutifully and religiously so that God will bless them and take their problems away. They seek to please others to appear pleasing. These people often "abandon" their own needs and problems to serve others. But because they don't understand that their own needs and desires still control their motivation, they become disappointed and bitter in their service.

The call to serve others does not paint a picture of men and women drained and empty, devoid of energy and enthusiasm. God's call to serve the church doesn't mean we should deny our legitimate human needs or all of the desires and passions that He has placed within us. Jesus took care of Himself physically and emotionally, and He challenged His followers to embrace their uniqueness and pursue the dreams God had given them. But like Jesus did, we must allow God to determine which needs are legitimate. This means yielding our desires and passions to His guidance and investing our energies in ways that build His kingdom.

Some people are simply self-absorbed, lost in their own problems and needs. "I can't serve others," they honestly admit, "because I am too messed up myself." Unfortunately, they never seek understanding of the deeper spiritual and emotional issues that fuel their root problems. Consequently, they remain trapped in their pain. No matter how bad the cards that have been dealt to you, however, you still can learn to give of yourself in service to God. Your pain can be powerfully transformed into purpose.

I know a woman who lived almost her entire lifetime in bondage, but she found the courage to change. She is now nearly 70, and about five years ago, she admitted that she had been sexually molested as a child. For decades, she had carried this secret around with her. She had trouble giving to others because of her own deep pain. By finally opening up about her problem to some people in the church, she was courageously saying that she would not settle for being a victim anymore. As she honestly worked through her pain, she began to discover God's healing grace. A year after sharing her secret, she began a ministry to help others who had been abused find the same freedom and fulfillment she was experiencing. She now ministers to more than 500 women through her outreach program.

Her sorrow was turned to joy as she watched others heal the same brokenness that was preventing them from knowing God's best.

That is the beauty of God's plan, the full circle of His redemptive love. Those in need are lovingly served and are slowly and gradually transformed by such love. Then they, too, can begin to serve others in need. And the cycle—once a destructive path of pain—becomes infused with the healing power of God.

Giving Back to God What Belongs to Him

God is a gift-giver who desires for us to use those gifts to serve Him. His plan is as natural as a river flowing into a sea. That is the simple beauty of God's design. But living in a country with so many things and so many opportunities, it is easy to lose sight of the fact that every gift is from God. We forget that everything belongs to God and we are simply stewards of what we've been given. Our materialistic, image-obsessed culture often keeps us from seeing things as we should.

As I mentioned earlier, before Sandy and I were married we went on a missions trip to India. The country is so poor that begging has been organized into networks called "begging rings." People in these organizations often maim and cripple their own children so they will appear more pathetic, generating more sympathy and, hopefully, money.

These deformed people grow up and find little else they can do to earn a living.

Many of these beggars congregate outside of the city in slums. I'll never forget the church service we attended in one of those slums, named Koramungala, which was little more than a collection of shacks made of wood scraps and cardboard. As we prepared for the service, we watched these poor, deformed people hobble up the street where open sewage was flowing around them. Slowly and with great care, they would make their way to the front of the shack that served as a church and give their money as an offering.

These people—deformed, impoverished, and rejected by the world—truly believed that everything they had was God's. To honor God, they wanted to give a portion (if not all) back to Him. These poor people had pure motivations for giving to God. They didn't give to get. They simply gave out of deep conviction that all gifts should return to the Giver.

Giving sacrificially to God cannot be just a "compartment" of our lives, like watching football on Sunday afternoon or preparing a budget. It should be the overriding passion of who we are. Everything we have—our money, time, energy, talents, hearts, and minds—should be returned to Him in love through serving others. This is not always easy, pleasant, or glamorous. You will probably never win an award or be featured on TV because of your service. A good deal of the service we do for others will be tedious and uninspiring.

My wife is someone who serves even when it is not glamorous to do so. Sandy has a love for her grandmother that is very rare, and each week she makes sure that "Nana" gets to spend time with Madeline, her only great-granddaughter and one of the only sources of joy in her life. Nana is 94 years old and has never been able to walk without a walker. Now she can't walk at all and needs constant care. My wife has taken great pains to find her the right care and to spend loving and consistent time with her. Although it is often monotonous, Sandy finds deep joy in knowing that she is giving back to her grandmother, who has given her so much.

⮜⮞

The book of Revelation says that there will be a great wedding feast for Jesus Christ and His bride, the church. Revelation 19:9 states, "Blessed are those who are invited to the wedding supper of the Lamb!" In my mind, I picture a huge reception hall, with golden tables and a 12-story cake studded with emeralds and sapphires. After the angels stop singing their wedding songs, the crowd will separate to allow Jesus to pass through to a table in the center of the room. On it are the gifts to the bride. Which ones will be yours?

THE PLACE OF PAIN

How SUFFERING REFINES OUR FAITH

It was the first night of our honeymoon. As I was driving to the airport to catch our airplane, which would take Sandy and me to our tropical paradise, I was thinking about how great it was going to be—not only our first night together, but also our marriage. Before long, however, I was pulled from my reverie by the sound of crying . . . from my wife.

Shocked, I looked at her and asked, "Honey, why are you crying?"

In between her sobs, she managed to say, "I'm afraid for you to take me out of town."

Just hours into our marriage, I felt a surge of panic.

Things only got worse. On the first day of our Club Med honeymoon, my wife was sitting on the beach next to a woman from California who was worried because she had not seen her husband for a while. Within the next few minutes, we all watched, horrified, as lifeguards dragged his body up from the bottom of the ocean. He was dead. The rest of the week, all the vacationers and honeymooners called the spot "Club Dead."

It was a depressing start to our wedded lives together. In some ways, the tragic honeymoon foreshadowed a dreadful first year of marriage.

At first, we simply assumed that we had married the wrong person. Little seemed right about our relationship, and each day brought with it some new difficulty or conflict. Of course, both of us thought the other person was completely at fault. We looked like we had our act together, but behind the facade, we were hiding a deep, painful secret about our relationship, one which we rarely talked about even with each other.

Ironically, we had joined a support group of four couples at church. The theory was that we would share our problems and help one another. Our group included a pastor and his wife, a baseball player and his wife, a government official and his wife, a psychologist and his wife, and us. What was designed to help facilitate authenticity became a sorry example of how people with big needs can hide them, even while meeting with each other face-to-face.

Week after week, Sandy and I went to this superficial group. Each couple shared only those things that were safe. It was like an adult game of hide-and-seek. All of us needed each other; in fact, two other couples had marriages that were in big trouble, too, but no one would risk the vulnerability required to be open, honest, and authentic.

One night as we were coming home, Sandy told me, "If we're going to belong to this group and spend this much time with them, we're going to share what's really going on in our lives."

I reluctantly agreed. So the next week we went back to the group committed to telling the truth.

When the sharing started, Sandy broke in and said, "It's time that we reveal what we're really dealing with. We've been married a year, and the sexual intimacy part of our marriage isn't working. You can count on one hand the number of times we've even tried to be intimate with each other. Both of us looked forward to this part of marriage, but it just hasn't happened."

I will never forget the looks on the faces of those people. It was as if we had just dumped a truckload of radioactive material into the living room. There was a lot of shifting in seats, coughing, and looking at the floor. They just didn't know what to do. Instead of creating an opportunity for all of us to be genuine, Sandy's honesty came as a threat. I think each member of the group instinctively knew that since we had revealed our own pain and struggle, we had earned the right to confront them about the true nature of their relationships. That was the last time that the group ever met. No one came back, and we were left feeling embarrassed and humiliated.

Hiding Behind Facades

Why is it that Christians, who are supposed to be committed to the truth, often seem to be the most fake people on earth? One reason is that we've been told—either outright or subtly—that Christians shouldn't struggle. The message is, if only we had enough faith, our conflicts and problems would resolve themselves. If we're good Christians, we'll have it all together. So we hide our struggles behind polished masks.

Many people expect that God will give them lives of ease and comfort once they accept Christ. This Sunday, from hundreds of church pulpits, a message will be preached: "If you will come to Christ, your problems will disappear because Christ is the answer. You will have a Christian home, and if you pray for your children, then they will grow up to be wonderful Christians, too, protected by the hand of God."

The problem is in how people twist the meaning of Christ's promise of joy. They believe it to mean living near-perfect lives, free from struggle and pain. I once saw a slick advertisement put together by the Mormon church. In it, a perfect couple, with perfect white teeth, holding a perfect child, were rowing across a perfect little lake on a perfect evening when the sun spread a perfect rose color across the water. The message, of course, was this: Become a Mormon and you, too, will have a perfect life. That may make for a good ad, but it sure won't translate into real life.

The same is true with the Christian faith. If you expect the Christian walk to be a stroll through the park, think again. Becoming a Christian does not remove struggle from your life; in fact, it often *adds* to the struggle or intensifies it. Some of the most committed Christians have lived some of the most difficult lives. The great theologian Dietrich Bonhoeffer said, "When Christ calls a person, he bids them come and die." Jesus never promised you a rose garden. When He stood with His frightened disciples after His resurrection, He showed them the scars on His hands and side. Then He told them, "As the Father has sent me, I am sending you" (John 20:21). The path that Jesus wants us to follow leads through the pain of the cross. In fact, He tells each of us to pick up our crosses and follow Him (see Luke 9:23).

As Christians, we do not have the option of running from pain and struggle. Pain is as much a part of this world as are beauty and free will. To pretend otherwise is to simply dismiss reality. As we saw in chapter 6, some people will go to unbelievable extremes to avoid pain. Unfortunately, this is true for many Christians. Like the people in the small group I described earlier, Christians hide behind facades, jargon, niceties, and rules. They lose themselves in the false hope that one day everything will be perfect. But because they are not dealing with the realities of life, they soon find themselves self-absorbed, without love for others or for God.

When we face the fact that the world is a messy place—that love is often tinged with betrayal, that children sometimes die of cancer, that dreams often end up shattered—then we can learn from that pain that we are helpless without God. And depending on God is the healthy outcome of pain.

Authentic Christianity

What does it mean to have an authentic Christian faith? What does it require? Some Christians act as though they have achieved a level of faith that places them above the tough realities of life. They lead us to believe they are "first-class" Christians who have found the secret to a near-perfect life, devoid of pain. This concept is not only wrong, it is toxic.

The authentic Christian life doesn't involve attaining perfection, and it doesn't mean living free from struggle; instead, it deals head-on with the issue of pain. Rather than trying to avoid pain, as authentic Christians we allow struggle to shape our hearts and our faith. We allow humility to draw us further out of ourselves and closer to God. It is not an easy life, but it is a rich life, full of growth and tough moments that remind us of who we are and how far we have to go in our spiritual journey. In the face of pain and struggle, our faith will give us comfort, guidance, and hope.

The biblical view of life is that it often gets worse before it gets better. Salvation, the free gift of God, is sometimes painful. Listen to the apostle Peter address the value of suffering:

> Now for a little while you may have had to suffer grief in all kinds of trials. These have come so that your faith—of greater worth than gold, which perishes even though refined by fire—may be proved genuine and may result in praise, glory and honor when Jesus Christ is revealed. Though you have not seen him, you love him; and even though you do not see him now, you believe in him and are filled with an inexpressible and glorious joy, for you are receiving the goal of your faith, the salvation of your souls. (1 Peter 1:6–9)

In Romans, Paul also describes this "refining process" of suffering: "We also rejoice in our sufferings, because we know that suffering produces perseverance; perseverance, character; and character, hope. And hope does not disappoint us, because God has poured out his love into our hearts by the Holy Spirit, whom he has given us" (Romans 5:3–5).

This, of course, does not mean we should act happy when we find out our leg has to be amputated or we have a terminal illness. It does mean that one day we will rejoice at the adversities we faced and the way Christ brought us through them.

In my own life, suffering has taught me some of the deepest lessons of faith. For seven years, my wife and I waited for a child. We prayed and prayed and begged God, but nothing happened. For seven long years, we did everything that the infertility doctors suggested, but nothing worked. With each passing month, our despair grew as we realized we would never have children.

Finally, through circumstances only God could have arranged, we were able to adopt our daughter, Madeline. She has become the light of our lives. This child is even more precious to us because we know she is a direct gift from God. Nothing we could have done would have brought Madeline to us.

Although the suffering seemed unbearable at times, the ordeal taught Sandy and me lessons we could not have learned otherwise. Pain can be a powerful teacher because it forces us to under-stand that change and struggle are a necessary part of the maturation process.

Can You Spare Some Change?
My parents were godly Christians. Yet suffering brought them face-to-face with change that they

never anticipated. Learning that their son was dying of AIDS forced them to see the difficult realities of life. Like many other Christians, they thought that if they honored God and dedicated their children to the Lord, we would be shielded from pain and suffering. They discovered, the hard way, that this belief was false.

God had allowed Jerry to contract AIDS after becoming involved in the homosexual lifestyle. My parents wrestled with not only losing Jerry, but also with feelings of guilt: What could they have done differently to keep their son from such deadly behavior? Their faith did not protect them from falling apart in a terrible mixture of sorrow and regret.

God used that terrible incident to mold and deepen their faith. When Jerry needed them most, my parents were able to display the courage and forgiveness necessary to lead him to repentance. They also developed deep compassion for others as a result of their suffering. Their hearts and lives were forever changed.

Change is always difficult, no matter what the situation entails. Most of us love the status quo. We often grow comfortable and choose to ignore aspects of our lives that need improvement. But sometimes God asks us to make adjustments in areas we would rather just leave alone. Sometimes He asks us to change a career; other times, it's a change in our perspective about money or priorities.

Change is never easy, especially after years of living a certain way. Responding to God's call to change can be painful because it often requires a transformation beyond what we thought possible. Nevertheless, what is impossible for us to achieve alone is possible through the power of God.

The End of Self

Sometimes our lives seem to get worse because God wants to show us that He is our only hope. If we can control something on our own, we will never come to know the greater power of God. God loves to step in and prove His faithfulness to us. No matter what the circumstances, God is still in control and will act according to His eternal plan. Isaiah 30:18 tells us the Lord is a God of justice for those who wait on Him. He will not abandon us in our times of helplessness. We must trust that He is able to change the worst situation into a time of hope and joy.

Donna lived with her husband and two babies on the $400-a-month pension he received from the navy. Their rent was more than $200 a month. Needless to say, the money often ran out. One month, their financial situation was so bad that Donna literally had no money left to buy laundry soap to wash her babies' dirty diapers.

Donna got on her knees in the kitchen and prayed, "God, I've never needed You like I need

You now. I have nothing, and I need You to provide soap to wash these diapers."

Hearing a noise at the front door, Donna got up and went to open it. Someone had left a sample of soap in a plastic bag on her doorstep. It was a promotional giveaway. But Donna knew better. In utter helplessness, she had cried out to God for help. Some would call the provision a coincidence, but Donna knew it was an act of God.

God wants us to see Him as our only real hope. Through the pain, God will act to show you that He cares for you personally and deeply. Rather than give up on Him, we must surrender faith in ourselves so we can tap into God's divine power.

God of the Impossible

When things appear to be most impossible, God can show us He is in control. Our trials can become landmarks on our spiritual journey. Mark 10:27 says, "With man [it] is impossible, but not with God; all things are possible with God." Countless people in the Bible faced "impossible" situations, only to be delivered by a loving God. Gideon's armies, greatly outnumbered, defeated their enemies. The Israelites, pinned against the Red Sea by a fierce Egyptian army, crossed to safety on dry land. Paul, imprisoned in a dark cell, was able to sing songs of praise. In our troubles, we must find the courage to believe that nothing is impossible with God.

One of my favorite verses in the Bible is John 11:39, which I like to paraphrase as, "He stinketh." If there is something in your life that stinks, just remember that Lazarus, four days dead, also reeked to high heaven. Even when all hope was gone, Jesus showed His remarkable power and love by resurrecting Lazarus. If He can do that, He can give you new life and hope.

Sharing the Sufferings of Christ

There is still another reason God often allows us to endure heartache. Sometimes He allows our lives to deteriorate into a dark chasm of pain because He wants us to share in the sufferings of Jesus Christ. As the apostle Paul said, "I want to know Christ and the power of his resurrection and the fellowship of sharing in his sufferings" (Philippians 3:10). This last reason is perhaps the most painful, but it also produces the greatest spiritual growth and understanding of God's nature.

If in some small way we can begin to understand the depths of suffering that Christ endured for us, then we will draw even closer to Him. In these agonizing times, we are invited to meet Jesus as a suffering savior who willingly endured great hardship, even the pain of crucifixion, because He loved us so much. We can only understand this suffering love if we share in the suffering with Him.

There have been painful times in my life when

I have had nothing to hold me up but the knowledge that Christ had suffered before me and was
suffering with me. These experiences have taught
me new dimensions of Christ's suffering love.

On April 1, 1995, my five-year-old daughter
and I set off for our first rides on brand-new bicy-
cles. Just past our house is a fork in the road: One
way leads up a steep hill; the other way leads down
an equally steep slope. Madeline and I approached
the fork and were preparing to go up. Riding
behind Madeline, I glanced down at my bike chain
for just a moment. When I looked back up, I was
horrified to see that she was beginning to roll *down*
the hill.

She was picking up speed and heading for
either a large metal Dumpster in front of a house
under construction or a six-foot drop-off onto a
concrete slab. Neither of those options would have
had a very pretty outcome. Judging by her speed, I
envisioned her ending up with a smashed-up face
and broken bones . . . or worse. I watched in horror
as she tried to figure out how to make the brakes
work. Unfortunately, one pedal was up and one was
down, and she didn't realize that she had to pedal
forward before she could be in a position to brake.
My precious little girl was on a runaway bicycle!

I knew I had to respond quickly. Jumping off
my bicycle, I sprinted after her. I was wearing only
a T-shirt, a pair of shorts, and some loafers. I ran

faster than I have ever run in my life. I ran so fast that I slipped out of my shoes. I ran so hard that the pavement severely bruised bones in my heels and soles, which took months to heal. I ran so swiftly that I seemed to be moving with supernatural speed.

I caught up with my daughter, and, seconds before she hit the Dumpster, I was able to lunge and grab her by the back of her sweater, veering her away from the huge metal monster. But we weren't out of danger. She and I and the bicycle crashed together and slid on the rough pavement. Fortunately, I somehow managed to get between her and the street.

When we came to a stop, Madeline untangled herself from the heap of metal, rubber, skin, and bones. As she stood up, I looked her over. She was perfectly intact, without a scratch. She looked at me and immediately began to cry when she saw that I was covered with blood. In her mind, I had just made it into the Owie Hall of Fame.

I had never experienced that kind of pain and blood loss. There were places on my feet that were scraped to the bone, which required a tetanus shot and antibiotics. I had taken a handlebar to my ribs and had pedal marks across my lower back. Twenty-three places on my feet, legs, knees, arms, and back were scraped, cut, and bruised from the pavement.

As I slowly stood up to assess the damage to my body, I almost couldn't breathe. I looked at Madeline again and then back down at my wounds, but rather than join her in her tears, a huge grin spread over my face. Seeing Madeline in such good shape, I realized I had sacrificed my body for someone I love. For the first time, I had saved someone I love dearly from pain. I was ecstatic in suffering love.

The experience gave me a new realization of Christ's love for me. I understood that His motive and willingness to die for me on the cross sprang from pure and undying love. That painful bicycle wreck made me more secure in my faith. I felt a fellowship with the Savior that I would not have known otherwise.

I don't know of anyone who gets excited about the possibility of their lives becoming more painful and difficult. We all want to stay on the easy path. Biblical history and even our own lives show that more often than not, when we accept God's truth, we are in for a tough journey that will require a deep faith if we are to endure.

Yes, when we respond to God, things often get worse before they get better. But God has promised that if we have trust in Him, He will turn our suffering into joy—and refine our faith in the process. With endurance, our lives and faith become deeper and richer.

CHAPTER FOURTEEN

CHRIST'S WOUNDS

THE CONSEQUENCES of HIS GRACE

Recently, I spoke at a church near Newark, New Jersey, on the concept of reproducing our sins in our children. A man came up to me afterward, deeply troubled. When he heard that the sins of the father could be passed on to the children, he was racked with guilt and fear because his past was so full of wrongdoing and rebellion. His father had been quite a sinner, and many of the things this man had done were a repeat of his father's indiscretions.

As I talked to him, though, I found one critical difference between his father and himself—he was remorseful about his sin, and his father never had been. I told him that because of his repentant heart, he had a great opportunity to be part of a transitional generation in his family. That is, he could be the one to break the chain of sin that had been passed down from generation to generation. He could accept Christ's free gift of healing and pass it on to his own children.

When we parted ways a few minutes later, this man left with renewed hope. He realized that his life was far from doomed. By God's grace, he was becoming a new man, a new creature, and he could set a godly example for his children.

Jesus Christ, the great healer, acts to set things right. In faith, we must allow His power to work within us to heal our wounds; if we don't, it's likely we will either ignore them or, worse, attempt to heal them ourselves. And sometimes in our pain we will venture back onto the broad path to find a quick and easy balm. This creates still more wounds, though.

Instead of letting our pain drive us into more sin, we should let it drive us to God. To repentance. To the hope of healing and new life. Once we honestly face the reality of our wounds, God honors our faith and leads us into a process of restoration. He literally takes all the junk we have inflicted on ourselves and turns it into a trophy of restoration. When we turn to Him in our failures, He weaves a tapestry of divine beauty in us.

In the previous chapters, I described the many times that I chose the wrong road. But thank God, He brought me back to Himself, back to the narrow path that leads to healing. I repented of my deadly choices. I confessed all of the times I chose paths that were not motivated by love. Nevertheless, I will often be tempted to leave God's path. I love how *The Message* paraphrases the apostle Paul's lament regarding his struggle with sin:

*The moment I decide to do good, sin is
there to trip me up. I truly delight in
God's commands, but it's pretty obvious
that not all of me joins in that delight.
Parts of me covertly rebel, and just when
I least expect it, they take charge. I've
tried everything and nothing helps. I'm
at the end of my rope. Is there no one
who can do anything for me? Isn't that
the real question? The answer, thank
God, is that Jesus Christ can and does.
He acted to set things right in this life of
contradictions where I want to serve
God with all my heart and mind, but
am pulled by the influence of sin to do
something totally different. (Romans 7)*

The path to healing and new life is so narrow
that we must follow the footsteps of Jesus as He
clears the way for us through the forest of sin and
certain death. Then, and only then, somewhere
along the path we will unexpectedly find ourselves
experiencing moments of true healing and abundant life.

The Birth of Hope
A word of caution: Restoration is often a slow
process. Sometimes it takes a lifetime. Perhaps it
will never fully happen until we reach heaven. We

must give the enormous power of sin its due; it never disappears with the wave of a magic wand. But the God of grace gives us second chances. In fact, I would like to tell how one of my self-inflicted wounds has been slowly and painfully healed.

The promiscuity of my early adult life—what I considered to be "free love"—ended up costing me dearly. Because sexual sin involves intense intimacy between two humans, it almost always has enduring consequences. There were times along the way when I thought that, through faith, I had achieved some measure of healing. But then the consequences would come back to haunt me, often in camouflaged forms. Like a virus that "disappears" and then re-emerges to cause more painful symptoms, my sexual sin has been a source of deep and often unexpected trouble.

Too often the powerful and continued consequences of sexual sin are downplayed. I never cease to be amazed by the pervasiveness of those consequences. Once, after speaking to more than 2,000 students at Baylor University, I was rudely brought to a new awareness of my depravity. My motivation for speaking was a good one: I wanted to help the young people avoid making the same mistakes I had made as a student there some 20 years before. I hoped to warn them about the consequences of sexual sin. I was the one, however, who was taught a powerful lesson.

After I was introduced by the chaplain, who had warned me not to let the students' inattention shake me, I began my speech. I would have loved to have stood before them as some big-shot or "alumnus made good," but I was compelled to honestly reveal who I was and what I had been through.

"I came to this school 20 years ago as a student to get a Christian education," I began, "but instead, I got a girl pregnant."

I listened to the rush of wind as all of the newspapers were folded and notebooks closed. I obviously got their attention. Even though it was not easy, I told them the truth: that I paid for half of the abortion costs; that, after all, was the least I could do to get rid of what I had considered a mere "inconvenience"; that I never stopped to think about what I was doing; that the realization that I had murdered my child almost cost me my life. Because of the guilt and inner turmoil, I'd had ulcers eating at my stomach, intestines, and colon.

What I experienced has been labeled male post-abortion syndrome, which is marked by the powerful guilt and shame that results when a person commits an act of genocide. The despair, emptiness, and pain are overwhelming. The guilt is often increased by the fact that the man, who is supposed to protect the mother and child after conception, has instead become a destroyer of life. I explained to the students that although male post-abortion syndrome is less traumatic than what the woman usually experiences, it is nonetheless real.

I also told them how I had struggled spiritually for two years before I could accept the forgiveness that was available to me through Christ. My life got worse before it got better. My physician told me that in order to live, I would either have to have surgery or something miraculous would have to change in my life. Accepting Christ's forgiveness was the only miracle I needed. As I began to heal spiritually, my physical condition improved as well. Over time, the internal scars disappeared, and tests by physicians in the years ahead would reveal no trace of the trauma.

As I gave my speech, I realized that if my child had been given the opportunity to live, she would have been about the age of these students and could have been in the audience. That thought grieved me. The speech had been tremendously draining, but I felt it was worth it. Several students lined up to talk with me afterward, many of whom struggled with secret sexual sins.

Shortly after giving my talk at Baylor, I received a phone call. It was from the girl I had gotten pregnant all those years ago. We talked for a while, and she told me God had also restored her, though not without much pain and struggle. Then she confronted me.

"The next time you tell the story," she said, "be more honest about what really happened."

I was confused. I thought I had been as honest as possible.

"What do you mean?" I asked.

She reminded me that I didn't just help pay for the abortion; I had *pressured* her to get it. She had never wanted to do it. She wanted to give birth to the baby and raise it or put it up for adoption. My forcefulness and manipulation led her to abort the child against her will. Once again, through the truth, the consequences of my sin painfully resurfaced.

That phone call forced me to see who I really am. Because of my cowardice, I had persuaded a wonderful person to assist me in ending a life. Facing the truth about myself wasn't a pleasant experience, but I needed to do it to complete the healing process.

A Cycle of Healing

The pattern of healing became a familiar one to me: truth, despair, repentance, healing. Each time I realized the truth about my sins and their consequences, the cycle repeated itself. I wish I could say that my problems ended with a single instance of repentance; they did not. Sometimes I would avoid the truth or slip away from my faith and revert to old patterns. Rather than face the truth about myself, I was always tempted to return to the broad and easy path of destruction. Relief seemed easier than healing; comfort was preferable to honesty.

The narrow path to grace seems inexpressibly difficult because acts of repentance and faith are painful. I gradually made my way back to a whole and healthy relationship with God, but not before I obtained counseling and worked through many issues with the help of an accountability group. Through this, I learned to live out my commitment to a God-honoring lifestyle.

It was at this time, after so much progress in my own life and in my marriage, that Sandy and I came to realize we couldn't have children. We had struggled with infertility for seven years, and it was clear that we would never be able to conceive. Sandy and I both were struck anew with sorrow, depression, and a sense of personal failure. The irony never escaped me: Once, when I could create life, I had ended it. Now I could not create it, even though I desperately wanted to.

Our emotional pain was compounded when some Christians suggested that our infertility was God's judgment. They concluded that my past sexual sin was now keeping us from having children. These insensitive and misguided remarks almost undid what I had finally resolved with God—that He does forgive and offer second chances. I have always found it amazing how other Christians can hold a grudge at the same time God offers grace.

The Surprise of Life

At times, the process that God took us through seemed unbearably difficult, almost cruel. Once, after I spoke at a crisis pregnancy center fund-raiser, a pregnant woman approached my wife and me and asked if we would want her baby. Although we hadn't talked much about adoption, we were instantly excited and pursued the process with her counselor. As it turned out, the counselor was upset with the woman because she had not consulted her, and she manipulated the woman into withdrawing her offer. Like thousands of others who are rejected in the adoption process, Sandy and I were devastated. It seemed as if God had placed a carrot in front of us, then removed it at the last second. It was simply too much for Sandy to bear, and after that incident we no longer considered adoption to be a viable option for us. We could not deal with that kind of rejection and pain again.

For another year, we remained mired in our quiet desperation. We had resigned ourselves to remaining childless. Then, in July 1990, I was asked to speak to a group of 4,000 black, charismatic Christians in Atlanta, Georgia, which was unusual because I am neither black nor charismatic. Somehow, I had arranged for Sandy to come along, which she rarely had the opportunity to do.

After I spoke, a woman approached me and said, "God has given me a message for you."

For a second, I squirmed: I had just bought a new car, and I thought maybe God was going to tell me to give it back. But that wasn't the case.

She continued, "The Lord told me that you are going to receive a gift—a baby."

I nodded politely and said, "Thank you for your concern, but I'm afraid my wife and I can't have children. We've gone through years of testing, and we're infertile."

That same day, July 3, 1990, I met my friend and publisher Victor Oliver for lunch. Unexpectedly, he inquired about our plans for children. I brought him up to date on our long struggle.

"Well," Victor said, "here's something to think about. My best friend's 16-year-old daughter is pregnant. She and her boyfriend have decided not to abort the child, and they're looking for a Christian couple to raise their baby. Would you be interested?"

The next day, Independence Day, Sandy and I met with the couple. We fell in love with them and marveled at their courage. They wanted their baby to have all the things they, being young and unestablished, knew they couldn't provide. This couple obviously loved their unborn child.

After much deliberation, they decided to give

us their baby. They phoned us with the news, and we began preparing the house and taking baby classes. Late Christmas Eve, we were awakened by a phone call with the news that the baby had been born. The next day, Christmas, we flew to Atlanta to meet our little girl. We spent the next couple of days with the baby's father as they made their final evaluations. When our baby was finally handed over, the nurse didn't give her to Sandy but placed her in my arms. What a moment! Never before or since in my life have I so powerfully understood God's amazing grace.

This young couple lovingly gave up their child so she could have the best possible life, and Sandy and I could have the best possible lives. These courageous people represent all who allow couples like us to become parents.

I, who for so long had struggled with my sin and our infertility, was handed this gift of new life. What a gracious and creative God! He had restored what I had so carelessly destroyed years ago. We knew that this kind of joy could only come from God.

The narrow path to restoration was difficult, but God's surprising grace was always there. He wanted what was best for me, so He allowed me to face the truth about myself, bringing me to real repentance. And in His perfect timing, He surprised me with His incredible grace—and the gift of life.

By His Wounds

In his remarkable book *The Wounded Healer*, Henri Nouwen tells us that Christ is able to heal us because He was wounded Himself. Isaiah 53:5 affirms this: "But he was pierced for our transgressions, he was crushed for our iniquities; the punishment that brought us peace was upon him, and by his wounds we are healed." Christ not only suffered from physical wounds that He received on His feet, hands, and side, but also from the spiritual and emotional wounds that are caused by sin. For every wrongdoing committed, every cry of despair, every hopeless moment, Christ has suffered. The Father allowed His Son, Jesus, to be wounded so that we might be healed, whole, and righteous. Our wounds are His wounds. That is how much He loves us.

To truly repent of sin is difficult work. It means giving up control and yielding to the grace and power of God. It means understanding the deadly and pervasive power of sin. We all face the temptation to run from this dangerous truth, but by doing so, we leave our wounds untreated. Whatever wounds you have, you can't heal them by pretending they are not there. It takes courage to face the truth, but eventually, in doing that, God will set us, our churches, and our world free.

A BEACON
TO THE
WORLD

How the Church
can surprise unbelievers
with God's grace

Once, I appeared on the *Geraldo!* show. I am fessing up: It was during the "talk show phase" of my life, when I thought it was cool to be on TV. (I've since changed my mind, due in part to some bad experiences.) The topic was religion, and I was there to promote one of my books. Being on the show fell into the "means-justifies-the-end" thinking. That is, I thought if I could be a positive spokesman for Christianity and get people to read the book, it didn't really matter what the venue was.

Geraldo opened the program by showing a film clip of Jimmy Swaggert. He was standing on a stage with tears rolling down his cheeks, saying, "I've sinned, and I'll never do it again."

Next came a clip of Geraldo interviewing Swaggert a few days after Swaggert's grief-ridden confession.

"Have you been healed of this problem?" asked Geraldo, sticking a microphone to the man's mouth as they stood in an airport.

The televangelist responded confidently, "Geraldo, I've been healed 1,000 percent."

After showing these clips, Geraldo turned to

me, the token Christian on the show. Leading up to a question, he recounted all of the ugly details: the pornographic magazines found under the front seat of Swaggert's car, the meetings in the desert with prostitutes, and so on.

"So, Mr. Arterburn, is this what passes itself off for Christianity?" Geraldo asked confidently.

I had a few seconds to respond before the commercial break. I told Geraldo and his audience, "Anyone who judges the entire church by the actions of this man would be making a grave mistake."

I don't bring up this incident to disparage Jimmy Swaggert or re-open old wounds—after all, I'm sure we'd all prefer to forget that terrible time when it seemed that scandals involving Christian figures surfaced every week. My point is, the world watches the church, and frequently they get the wrong impression of what Christianity is all about. This sentiment was captured by Geraldo's question: "Is this what passes itself off for Christianity?"

Of course, it's not only highly visible people, such as TV preachers, who are closely watched to see what the Christian faith is all about; it's all of us who proclaim our faith in Jesus Christ. You and I may not get the media scrutiny that people like Swaggert do (thank goodness), but we're still observed by coworkers, neighbors, acquaintances, and family members.

If we want to reach the world for Jesus Christ,

Christians must begin to *live* as Jesus did. Unless we show Christ in our lives, the truth will remain dormant, and the church will lack the power that God desires for it to have.

How Is Your Faith "Packaged"?

I worry about the church. Recently, I attended a Christian retailers' conference and walked the aisles to see what Christians are selling to one another. Here is a partial list:

- *Christian pencils with cow-shaped erasers inscribed with "The Lord Moos Me."*

- *A machine that makes cross-shaped, cream-filled donuts. (I wonder, does this come in glazed and buttermilk versions?)*

- *Christian potpourri. (What makes it Christian, I don't know. Perhaps it smells like frankincense and myrrh.)*

- *The "Bless You" cookie. (It's similar to a fortune cookie, only the messages come not from Confucius but from God Himself. To preserve integrity, the cookie is made only from natural ingredients mentioned in the Bible. I've eaten these cookies, and they taste like ancient manuscripts.)*

Maybe I should learn to lighten up a little, but I find these kinds of presentations of the gospel offensive. The church should be in the business of living and proclaiming the active, supernatural, dynamic Word of God, not dispensing silly things that undermine the seriousness of the Bible. These days, the church often reduces God and His message to fit into safe and gift-wrapped boxes of faith. Do we see the power of God unleashed in this world? Do we see men like Daniel, who stood with courage and integrity to speak the undiminished truth of God? We don't often hear of people who sound like Nebuchadnezzar, the ancient king of the most powerful nation in the world, who was brought to his knees in worship: "I, Nebuchadnezzar, praise and exalt and glorify the King of heaven, because everything he does is right and all his ways are just" (Daniel 4:37).

What has gone wrong with the church? I am afraid that, without even realizing it, Christians are traveling along the world's broad paths—even as we *believe* we're on God's narrow path. And since the world cannot see an active and dynamic church, it no longer looks for God. Instead of seeing the all-powerful God of grace at work in our lives, the world often sees Christianity as just another religion that's irrelevant to the dealings of everyday life. Is it any wonder that people are so confused about God and the church?

I believe that when most people renounce Christ and His truth, they are actually rejecting the caricature of Christ that the church often presents. It is no wonder that a hurting and sick world looks elsewhere to find hope, comfort, relief, and freedom.

The Light of the World?

Jesus calls the church to be a beacon to the world: "You are the light of the world. A city on a hill cannot be hidden. Neither do people light a lamp and put it under a bowl. Instead they put it on its stand, and it gives light to everyone in the house. In the same way, let your light shine before men, that they may see your good deeds and praise your Father in heaven" (Matthew 5:14–16). But how can Christians be light to a dying world when we, too, are often full of darkness?

How we attempt to resolve this paradox is critically important to our Christian faith. Many Christians just don't deal with it. They simply move through life pretending to have it together and ignore anything that does not line up with their image of Christianity. But inside, they become filled with restlessness, anger, or apathy.

It's tempting to live in denial. We don't have to deal with hard problems, which present us with real pain. We'd rather believe that, with just the right amount of effort, we can make a good appearance on our own. So we buy self-help books, attend seven-steps-to-success seminars, and pray eloquently at baby dedications. By believing that appearances are what really matter, we walk the broad paths of destruction. As 2 Timothy 4:3–4 states, "For the time will come when men will not put up with sound doctrine. . . . They will turn their ears away from the truth and turn aside to myths." We must return to the truth by first rejecting lies. Colossians 2:8 reinforces this idea: "See to it that no one takes you captive through hollow and deceptive philosophy, which depends on human tradition and the basic principles of this world rather than on Christ."

And this is the truth: By ourselves, we are hopeless sinners. What God wants from us is not a denial of wounds but for us to honestly recognize our sin. The Bible calls this "living in the light" (see 1 John 1 and 2). I love the way 1 John 1:7 spells out the process: "But if we walk in the light, as he is in the light, we have fellowship with one another, and the blood of Jesus, his Son, purifies us from all sin." Notice the progression:

□ *Our sin is exposed by walking in the light;*
□ *We have fellowship with each other;*
□ *Our sin is purified by the blood of Jesus.*

As humans, we tend to hide from the light of exposure. The truths that we learn there are simply too terrifying. The Gospel of John expands on this truth:

> *This is the verdict: Light has come into the world, but men loved darkness instead of light because their deeds were evil. Everyone who does evil hates the light, and will not come into the light for fear that his deeds will be exposed. But whoever lives by the truth comes into the light, so that it may be seen plainly that what he has done has been done through God. (3:19–21)*

Coming into the light is not just a one-time thing we do, as in a point of conversion, but a constant process that is ignited and sustained through true biblical community. When we love one another, we are not to hide our weaknesses; instead, we must shine the light of God's Word into each other's hearts, exposing sin, so that it can be purified through the blood of Christ.

Far too often, we place barriers in front of the church. We don't like dealing with untidy people who have untidy problems. It makes us nervous. But we must never forget our own failings. And we must, with compassion and grace, reach out to those who are hurting or trapped in sin. Bound by love, we must meet people where they are. To reach the world, to set it free, our churches and its leaders need to create an environment of hope, acceptance, and loving accountability.

Be a Part of the Church

God wants you to participate in His church. And His church is made up of the most exciting and dynamic people in the world. You don't have to be a superstar or possess great talent or be very cute or even have a great past. The only requirement is to have an open and forgiven heart.

One of my favorite churches is Calvary Chapel, Capistrano Beach, which is near my home in California. The church, which is quite large and full of healthy Christians seeking a closer relationship with God, was not started because the pastor decided he wanted to be in charge of a big church. In fact, it was just the opposite. Chuck, the pastor, didn't even want to be a minister; he was planning on doing something completely different. But a group of people in south Orange County started praying for someone to lead their Bible study. After much prayer, the group called Chuck and asked if he would be willing to teach them. Chuck responded to their call.

Today, 20 years later, the church has ministered to many diverse people, who would normally never be caught dead in a church. In looking back, Chuck Smith, Jr. cringes when he thinks of what would have happened if he had not humbly accepted the call of God to be a pastor.

You may not be called to be a pastor, but you can participate in a dynamic ministry that God has uniquely designed you to do. When we ask God to use our talents and gifts, we find fulfillment in being directed by Him. Our prayers and our lives change. As we humbly submit to His will, we honor Him with our lives, and we become free—free to give.

Supernatural Love

When we unleash the power of the church, we can perform supernatural acts through the love and grace of God. While I have never seen God in person, I believe I have seen evidence of His direct working in my life and the lives of others. I could tell a thousand stories to show how God has worked through the church, but I will present just this one.

Fae was a Christian who had been married and divorced twice. The third time she got married, she also got pregnant. She decided to abort the child. But before the procedure, she decided to talk with Lisa, a friend who was an actress as well as a committed Christian.

"Pray for me," Fae told Lisa over the telephone. "I'm going in tomorrow to have an abortion."

Lisa responded in love. "I'm going to have my church pray for you. We're going to pray that you don't have that abortion."

That afternoon, Lisa gathered her prayer group together to pray about the situation. They prayed diligently, but Fae had the abortion anyway. Lisa and her group continued to pray that some good would come of the difficult circumstance.

Two days later, a nurse at the abortion clinic called Fae.

"We need you to come down here and talk with us," she said.

When Fae arrived, the nurse said, "We've done thousands of abortions, and this has never happened before. But we were studying the fluids from your procedure. We didn't get a lot of embryonic tissue there. Now we need to do a sonogram to see what happened."

They hooked up Fae to the monitors. On the screen, there was still a fetus there. The heart was beating.

The nurse then said, "We're terribly sorry, but we've got to go back in and finish the procedure."

"No," Fae said. "I believe this is one child that God wants to be born."

She had a little boy. Today, her child is alive and well because God can even abort an abortion as He works supernaturally through the church.

Rather than band together in prayer for the kingdom of God, we often demand God's power to further our own wish list. How different this world would be if we humbly petitioned God with requests on behalf of others. Not all of our prayers are answered with divine intervention or a supernatural outcome. But all of our prayers are answered and the outcomes are exactly what God wants them to be. It is important that we recognize that He is in control, not us. It is vital that we surrender to a God who can even abort an abortion.

The Authentic Church

As I have traveled around, I have had the great opportunity to speak in some wonderful churches. I attend one now. Sadly, this has not always been the case. Many of us were raised to believe that we must not embarrass the church or ourselves by revealing our sins. We are, instead, allowed to fudge a little on the truth, if it makes the church look better and its people more perfect. I was taught that the church was where hurting people came to hide, lest anyone think they may be lacking in their faith. I thought God was a faker since that was what I was used to in church.

It was a great surprise, then, to find that God's true vision of the church is for hurting, vulnerable, sinning, and sick people to come together to heal in the midst of the Holy Spirit. God never hid the realities of His family. The disciples, after walking with Christ Himself, doubted Him, lied about knowing Him, betrayed Him, and got into some of the most egotistical conversations ever recorded. The physical presence of Jesus did not produce perfection in the hearts of His disciples. Why should we expect perfection from ourselves?

God works with those who are authentic in their faith. They don't fake it because they have no need to. What they look like to God means more than what they look like to people. Revealing their own struggles and encouraging others to reveal theirs is more important than protecting themselves from the attacks of vicious gossips who lurk about in the hallways of every spiritually dead church.

God wants a real church with real people who are brave enough to face the truth about themselves and humble enough to share it with others. When that happens, the life of the church begins. Dead churches are playing hide-and-seek. Vibrant churches are safe places for people to be nothing more or less than who they really are. No revival ever ripped through a church, town, or country without at least one brave soul who decided to stop faking it and start coming out into the open about his condition. If you want to lead the charge for Christ, lead out into the open. Lay your heart bare for others to examine, and you will be surprised what God can do with you and those who follow your lead.

Conclusion

The surprise of infinite grace is a life-changing surprise. It is the motivation that keeps me going and trying to tell as many people about it as I can. It is my only hope—otherwise, I would face a life of certain condemnation because I know I am not good enough to earn my way to heaven. Except for God's grace, I just don't have what it takes. If you do not know this about God, if you are leading a life under condemnation, I invite you to the banquet table of our Lord who wants to fellowship with sinners like you and me. Please take a Bible and do a study on God's grace until you are certain you can feel it in your soul. You will be surprised at what God will do through you when you start responding to His grace rather than your failures.

That's it. I finished this book of the second chances God has given me. I am so grateful that you read this book and trusted me to introduce you to some of them. If God has given you some second chances that mean a lot to you, I would love to hear from you. You can reach me by writing to: Stephen Arterburn, Box 5009, Laguna Beach, California 92651.

A final note: One of the greatest joys of my life over the past few years has been to meet the people who run crisis pregnancy centers, adoption agencies, and those who fight for the lives of the unborn. Please support these organizations and centers with your prayers, your volunteer time, and your money. They need our support to turn tragedies into triumphs, to turn a crisis into an opportunity for God's healing grace and surprising power of restoration.

NOTES

Chapter 2

1. See Steve Arterburn and Jack Felton, *Toxic Faith* (Nashville: Thomas Nelson, 1991).
2. Ibid.
3. For further information on the "prosperity gospel" and other misguided forms of religion, see *Toxic Faith*.

Chapter 6

1. Dallas Willard, *The Spirit of the Disciplines* (San Francisco: Harper & Row, 1988).

Chapter 7

1. Anastasia Toufexia, "The Right Chemistry," *Time* (February 14, 1993).

Chapter 11

1. See Viktor Frankl, *Man's Search for Meaning* (New York: Simon & Schuster, 1984).

Also by Stephen Arterburn
**An Indispensable Handbook No Parent
Should Be Without**

Teens of the '90s face incredible pressures from
their peers and the "do-what-feels-good" society in
which we live. Guard your kids against such reckless behaviors as alcoholism, drug addiction,
promiscuity, and suicidal tendencies with *Parents
Guide to Top 10 Dangers Teens Face*.

Packed with proven principles, this practical
resource by Stephen Arterburn and Jim Burns
emphasizes the importance of establishing loving
and supportive boundaries when guiding youth
around life's potholes. By learning to notice—and
heed—the warning signs, you'll not only ward off
potential problems for your children, but also cur-
tail bad habits that are gaining momentum. Direct
your kids down the road to success with *Parents
Guide to Top 10 Dangers Teens Face* today!

Previously released as *When Love Is Not Enough*
and *Steering Them Straight*

If you are struggling with a problem from your past or present, please call 1-800-NEW-LIFE and allow a trained counselor to help you find God's power for restoration, renewal, and spiritual transformation.

To receive information about Stephen Arterburn's speaking schedule, please call (714) 376-0707.

More Faith-Strengthening Stories
From Focus on the Family®

Gianna
by Jessica Shaver

Gianna wasn't supposed to be here. Her frightened, 17-year-old mother went to an abortion clinic to end the life of the baby within her. But, miraculously, the procedure failed and sent Gianna's mother into labor and, a few minutes later, a fragile baby girl made her way into the world. The remarkable story of Gianna's survival is both inspirational and unforgettable. Paperback.

Too Young to Die
by Gordon McLean

Why are kids drawn to gangs? What can you do to protect your child from their influence? In *Too Young to Die*, former gang members reveal how gangs work and what compels kids to join. Their stories show that while the appeal of gang life is strong, the love of God is stronger and able to reach the hardened hearts of teens involved in a dangerous dead-end lifestyle. Paperback.

Look for these special books in your Christian bookstore or request a copy by calling 1-800-A-FAMILY (1-800-232-6459). Friends in Canada may write Focus on the Family, P.O. Box 9800, Stn. Terminal, Vancouver, B.C. V6B 4G3 or call 1-800-661-9800.

Visit our Web Site (www.family.org) to learn more about the ministry or find out if there is a Focus on the Family office in your country.

FOCUS ON THE FAMILY®

Welcome to the Family!

It began in 1977 with the vision of
Dr. James Dobson, a licensed psychologist
and author of best-selling books on
marriage, parenting, and family.
Alarmed by the many pressures
threatening the American family, he
founded Focus on the Family, now an
international organization dedicated
to preserving family values through the
life-changing message of Jesus Christ.

• • •

For more information about the ministry,
or if we can be of help to your family, simply
write to Focus on the Family, Colorado
Springs, CO 80995 or call 1-800-A-FAMILY
(1-800-232-6459). Friends in Canada may
write Focus on the Family, P.O. Box 9800, Stn.
Terminal, Vancouver, B.C. V6B 4G3 or
call 1-800-661-9800. Visit our Web
site at *www.family.org*.

We'd love to hear from you!